Felipe Portinho

Brazilian bass grooves/Rio de Janeiro

AF319534

Felipe Portinho

Brazilian bass grooves/Rio de Janeiro

The History of the Rhythmic Section in Brazil

ScienciaScripts

Imprint

Any brand names and product names mentioned in this book are subject to trademark, brand or patent protection and are trademarks or registered trademarks of their respective holders. The use of brand names, product names, common names, trade names, product descriptions etc. even without a particular marking in this work is in no way to be construed to mean that such names may be regarded as unrestricted in respect of trademark and brand protection legislation and could thus be used by anyone.

Cover image: www.ingimage.com

This book is a translation from the original published under ISBN 978-620-2-80389-2.

Publisher:
Sciencia Scripts
is a trademark of
International Book Market Service Ltd., member of OmniScriptum Publishing Group
17 Meldrum Street, Beau Bassin 71504, Mauritius
Printed at: see last page
ISBN: 978-620-2-81728-8

Copyright © Felipe Portinho
Copyright © 2020 International Book Market Service Ltd., member of OmniScriptum Publishing Group

DEDICATORY

I dedicate this work to Ana Beatriz Correa de Azevedo, Professor Eduardo Monteiro, Professor Paulo Henrique Loureiro de Sá, musicologist Flávio Silva and my students, may luck always watch over them!

SUMMARY

PORTINHO, Felipe Clark. **Brazilian rhythms on bass/Rio de Janeiro**. Dissertation (Professional Master in Music). School of Music, Federal University of Rio de Janeiro, Rio de Janeiro, 2017.

This research is based on interviews - which originated the documentary RITMOS BRASILEIROS NO CONTRABAIXO - whose objective is to show the adaptation of the bass to Brazilian genres since the appearance of the first orchestrations in the 1930s until the 1970s. It also sets the scene of the musical environment in the 19th century that provided the creation of genres such as Choro, Samba and later Bossa-Nova and compares them with their respective later modes of playing. Finally, it addresses the interviewees with questions aimed at clarifying the ethnic and timely contributions that resulted in the formation of various genres of Brazilian popular music.

Keywords: Double bass. Brazilian Popular Music. Rio de Janeiro. Choro. Samba. Bossa-Nova. Music in Brazil.

SUMMARY

INTRODUCTION

In January 2015 I was at the College of Charleston in South Carolina, United States, where Professor Frank Duval invited me to teach a Masterclass on Brazilian music. I accepted on the condition of speaking to Americans about the musical trajectory from the colonial period to Bossa Nova. To my surprise, the class that would only be for bass students in the last hour had to be redirected to a larger auditorium because of overcrowding. There, in front of a big audience and outside of my country, I could notice the enormous demand for information about our music both in the pedagogical and historical area, and particularly directed to my instrument, the double bass. Returning to Brazil I knew of the then recent death of one of the icons of our art, the guitarist Zé Menezes. I had from then on the idea of making a documentary about how these artists played at the beginning of the formations with the bass at the base of the ensembles and how they did to build an aesthetic and apply it in practice. I also wanted to hear from writers and musicologists a reasonable explanation for the appearance, still in the 19th century, of the vectors that brought about this whole scenario that would explode in the 1930s with the radios. From this came the research on **Brazilian Rhythms on Double Bass/Rio de Janeiro,** which is a textual transcription of the statements made in the documentary (the script of the documentary being transcribed), a work of exploratory, phenomenological survey, Therefore, with applied qualitative research (it intends to show how musicians did and how they do to play these genres) and consists in revealing, with a vast base of testimonies, both from scholars of the subjects referring to the 19th and early 20th century and from musicians who had contact with the pioneers, the following facts between 1808 and the 1970s: how these genres appeared in Rio de Janeiro; what were the social and economic vectors that triggered them still in the 19th century; what were the main protagonists of these events; how the development of the performance of the instruments on the part of the bass counterpoints, such as ophicleide, tuba, seven-string guitar and, finally, the bass. As the musicians of the rhythm section, mainly bassists and drummers, from the 1930s on, they adapted these genres to these formations - jazz combo, which is piano, bass and drums as a trio only or as a base for larger instrumentations.

I divide this research into four chapters. Chapter 1: The Prehistory of Brazilian Rhythms, which addresses the musical vectors still in the 19th century. Chapter 2: Pixinguinha and The First Bass Lines, which discusses the facts of the late 19th century until the recording of "Pelo Telefone" in 1917 - the first two recordings (that of the band and that of Bahiano) must have been made in early 1917[1] - and the transition from mechanical to electrical recording and

---

[1] Information sent to me by musicologist Flavio Silva in an e-mail dated May 7, 2017.

its consequences on the recent creation of radios. Chapter 3: Radamés, the Inventor of the Future, which will raise the facts that trigger the "phenomenon" Radamés Gnattali and the aesthetics of the "Radio Age in Brazil" and finally chapter 4: Bossa-Nova and the 1970s.

Two books structured this research, whose theoretical reference used since the beginning was **Brazilian Rhythms and their Percussion Instruments** (1962) - Rocca, Edgar Nunes - Rio de Janeiro - Escola Brasileira de Música, and another book with which I had contact in the course and served as an example of formatting: **The Mastery of Music: Ten Pathways to True Artistry** (2003) - Green, Barry - Broadwaybooks, and the latter helped me to define the dynamics of the dialogues, as it was exactly an exploratory survey based on statements, as in a documentary.

1. THE PREHISTORY OF BRAZILIAN RHYTHMS[2]

For the anthological drummer **Wilson Das Neves**[3] *"everything is samba!*

> **Maestro André Cardoso:** "The music scene at the arrival of Dom João VI is from a colony, in a country far away from Europe, which receives the court and the king himself, who was a person who cultivated and had an interest in music. The colony found itself in need of creating a structure to receive these people (from the court). Brazil, for instance, receives a great amount of musicians because the King then organized what could be considered the first state orchestra of the country, the Orchestra of the Royal Chapel that, on the one hand, had the obligations with the sacred music and, on the other hand, made what was called Royal Chamber that in the Palace of the Palace, where today is the Quinta da Boa Vista, practiced chamber music. At the same time there was a great tradition in the Portuguese court linked to Italian music, specifically to opera. Many composers left Portugal and went to Italy to make their musical formation especially in the city of Naples. Then, one of the needs was to build an Opera Theatre where this art could be practiced. Then it is created in 1813 the Theatro São João, where today it is the Teatro João Caetano (in the square Tiradentes in the centre of Rio de Janeiro). This is a period where many foreign musicians are received, mainly Portuguese and Italian and Rio de Janeiro starts to receive all kind of musicians from Europe who often stay for long periods in the capital. This generated a great artistic exchange and an update of the music that was made here. The main composer of the country, who was Father José Maurício, changes his way of writing because of this new demand, very different from what was practiced before 1808 and counting on a very present vocal virtuosity".[4]

In order to talk about the Brazilian rhythms on the double bass we have to explain where these genres and rhythmic variations came from, which for some musicians are simply diverse forms of the same genre, as mentioned above by *Wilson Das Neves*, and for others are popular manifestations that suffered syncretism with the people who arrived here.

Pedro Álvares Cabral and the Portuguese who arrived in Brazil following the discovery seem to have little to do with the music and musical genres of today in the country. But to arrive at the scenario that can set us in a "prehistory" of these genres - Choro, Samba and Bossa-Nova - in this research we will divide Brazilian history into before and after the Napoleonic Wars[5] and the arrival of the king of Portugal in Rio de Janeiro in 1808. Before Brazil colony had its own music[6] and it is also the basis of what will come before Choro and Samba in Rio de Janeiro, etc. It is also clear that in each of the economic cycles there was some musical representation

---

[2] This chapter of the documentary can be seen at: < https://www.youtube.com/watch?v=x9XxTeYICC4&feature=youtu.be>.

[3] Interview filmed with Wilson das Neves on the afternoon of August 14, 2016 in the neighborhood of Jardim Guanabara, Rio de Janeiro.

[4] Interview with Prof. Dr. André Cardoso at the Municipal Theater of Rio de Janeiro on the afternoon of August 17, 2016.

[5] As Maestro André Cardoso quotes in the statement just above about the arrival of the royal family in Rio de Janeiro.

[6] As will be mentioned below, in the testimony of the musicologist Flávio Silva in the e-mail sent to me on December 27, 2016.

in the Brazilian captaincies, some with records in musical notations and which were later duly compiled and even recorded in modern records through brilliant works of restoration and recovery of this cultural heritage, such as the recovery of the Mariana Archives[7] - a very important mining town in the Brazilian gold cycle. This colonial musical culture generated a whole lineage of artists that in Rio de Janeiro culminated in figures like Father José Maurício in the 19th century and the musicians who received the king of Portugal at the time of his arrival in the city of Rio de Janeiro.

I take advantage of the theme to bring the rhetoric sent to me by musicologist Flávio Silva, an important collaborator of this research, with criticism to the exclusion of the years of Brasil Colônia, a unique period to explain the causes of the "corruption of the modal ear" and the definition of "popular music" that we know today and emphasizing that all this happens well before that date of 1808. His vision in the e-mail sent to me already summarizes all the problems and sets us with rare mastery at the then arrival of the court, helping in our line of reasoning. wrote Flávio Silva[8]:

Flávio Silva (musicologist): "I think, however, that starting everything with the coming of the court is a very radical cut. The tone of the popular ear was commanded, well before that, by the sacred music of the colonial period, which spread throughout practically the whole country, of course with more intensity in the coastal area to reach a certain splendour in the Gerais. Without this corruption of the modal ear operated by tonalism we would not have José Maurício, who is a kind of quintessence of this aural transformation. The modinhas and lundus of the early 19th are already perfectly tonal.

In the US, segregationism has separated white people's churches from those of 'Christianised' blacks. Whites composed religious music for whites, blacks composed religious music for blacks, while in Brazil the mulattos became the creators of the 'white' music made in white churches for the same services. So in the U.S. there was no white sacred music composed by mulattoes; segregated blacks created their own sacred music, mixing tonalisms with African heritages. Thus popular religious music was created in the U.S. with a strength and drama that finds no parallel with any Brazilian religious music -- Catholic chants are of overwhelming piety. There is something interesting about umbanda, but candomblé is another story -- it's not popular music, it's cultured music.

There is another much more complicated issue which concerns the very idea of popular music. In my view, it is a consolidated European creation from the 17th century. I explain myself: in Asia and Africa, we have classical music/cultures based on theoretical systems explicitly formulated in written treaties, some of them even with embryonic notations, and traditional music under the total domain of orality, where theorisations were not explicitly formulated or organised, which does not mean that these songs did not have organised systems, but that organisation was not explicit. Both cultured and traditional songs were based on modal systems. These traditional songs are equivalent to what has been called folk music in Europe, to designate modal peasant songs, also practised in the urban environment. The consolidation of tone in European cultured music and the spread of the musical press, made more and more

---

[7] The work can be read and heard at the link of the Museum of Music of Mariana: <http://www.wikiwand.com/pt/Museu_da_M%C3%BAsica_de_Mariana#>.
[8] In an e-mail sent to me on 27 December 2016.

uniform and cheap, contributed to corrupting the traditional folk modal ear, which even led to the abandonment of traditional musical instruments, at first by urban populations, then by peasants. These instruments were replaced by those that had been perfected in order to be able to perform tonal music to their satisfaction. The role of the musical press is vital in this process. An increasingly diverse European middle class is being created which, in the lower strata, was not comfortable with the subtleties of 'noble' music and will increasingly want to create its own music, which was neither that of the upper stratum nor that of the peasantry. And so it was that what would be called popular music emerged in an urban setting, using tonal language, its instrumental, but abandoning the great forms to settle in the small ones, above all benefiting singing and dancing. In other words: this urbanised popular music stems from erudite music, contrary to what is generally claimed".

1.1 The Prehistory of Brazilian Rhythms

The double bass is an instrument that was present in Brazilian music with certainty at least since the beginning of the 19th century with the records that we have of the life of the musician Lino José Nunes[9] (? - Rio de Janeiro 1847) and his *Practical Method or Complete Studies for the Double Bass* of 1838. But the first historical record of the double bass in popular music appears in the 1912 photo that we can see in page 27 of this dissertation where we will deepen more in the counterpoints of the low voice. The important thing for us in this first chapter is to understand the impact on the musical life of Rio de Janeiro with the arrival of the court of Dom João VI.

---

[9] "This is probably one of the first methods for string instruments written in Brazil and presents a set of small lessons that can be placed in the category of studies for solo instruments. The work becomes more relevant because of the characters involved in its creation as author and dedicator. The author of the work, Lino José Nunes, a musician who lived in Rio de Janeiro between the end of the 18th century and the first half of the 19th century, and studied with Father José Maurício Nunes Garcia in the free course that he kept in his residence. As his disciple, he joined the choir of the Royal Chapel". Quote from André Cardoso. A Brazilian method of double bass, from the XIX century (1838): Lino José Nunes - Revista Brasileira de Música - Programa de Pós-Graduação em Música - Escola de Música da UFRJ - v. 24, n. 2, p. 437-442, Jul./Dec. 2011 - p. 426.

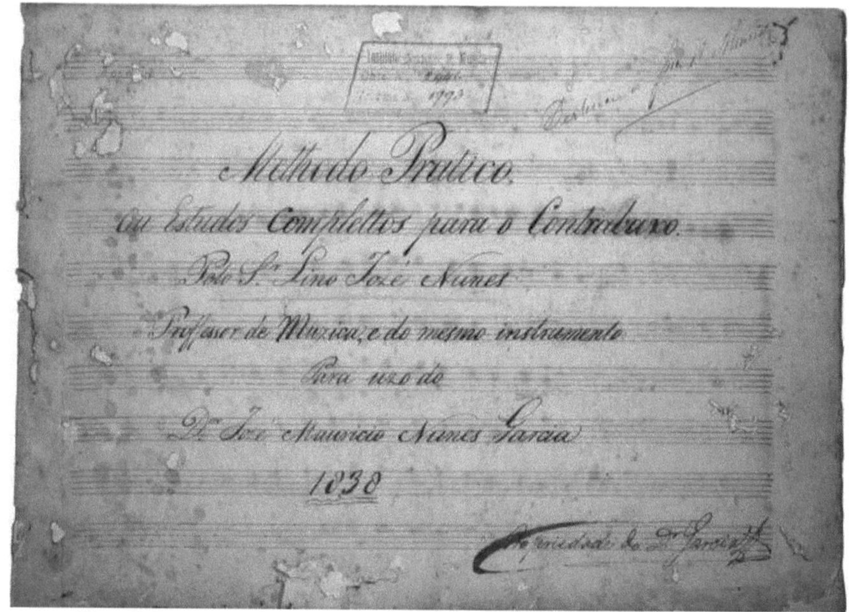

Figure 1: Frontispiece of the musical manuscript - Alberto Nepomuceno Library, EMUFRJ.[10]

About the change generated by the arrival of the King of Portugal in Brazil, fleeing Napoleon's persecution in 1808, the maestro and teacher André Cardoso, former artistic director of the Municipal Theatre of Rio de Janeiro, author of the book "A Música na Corte de D. João VI - 1808-1821", gives us the following example:

> **Maestro André Cardoso:** "Even the country's principal composer, Father Jose Maurice, changes his way of writing because of this new demand, very different from what was practiced before 1808 and counting on a very present vocal virtuosity".

Professor Henrique Cazes corroborates the fact:

> **Professor Henrique Cazes:** "Here what has not happened elsewhere (in the Americas) has happened. Why was it different here and why did it generate a music with these grandiose characteristics of choro, a music that is 150 years old and continues to renew itself? Because here in 1808 a court arrived. The royal family brought important teachers like the great flutist Matthieu André Reichert[11], the clarinetist Sigismund von Neukomm[12] and many others that were here in that period

---

[10] Frontispiece of the musical manuscript *Practical Method or Complete Studies for Double Bass*. Alberto Nepomuceno Library, UFRJ School of Music.

[11] *Matthieu or* Matheus André Reichert (Brussels, 1830 - Rio de Janeiro, 1880).

[12] Sigismund von Neukomm (Salzburg, 1778 - Paris, 1858).

and participated in the formation of a base, of a technical upholstery, that gave to those musicians here, even the popular ones, the possibility to coexist with a type of virtuosity, to coexist with more sophisticated things in terms of music than it happened, for instance in Santiago de Cuba or in New Orleans or in Martinique".[13]

About the centrality of Rio de Janeiro and the extensive visit of great European musicians during the reign of Dom João VI and then in the first and second empire comments André Cardoso:

André Cardoso: "In fact there was a centrality of Rio de Janeiro, especially because it was the capital of the country, to where things converged, all those travelers of the 19th century arrived at the port of Rio de Janeiro, so in a certain way Rio de Janeiro assumed a leading role in the music of Brazil that spread throughout the rest of the country. If you see that what we understand today as a reference of Brazilian music abroad is samba, choro and later bossa-nova, already in the middle of the 20th century, are essentially Carioca genres...".

"... we have already seen the example of Sigismund von Neukomm, a clarinettist, we can highlight Mathieu André Reichert, who was a virtuoso flutist and who wrote here part of his work, this one that goes in the genre that is between the most genuine popular music and classical music. That genre for entertainment from which originates a good part of popular music, especially the instrumental one that has choro as an example. Other musicians passed by here, for example: Louis Moreau Gottschalk, who died in Rio de Janeiro and wrote the famous variations of the national anthem (in the first empire of Dom Pedro I - 1798-1834)".

1.2 Samba and Crying

Figure 2: Maxixe.[14]

---

[13] Interview with Prof. Henrique Cazes in the studios of the Pocket Orchestra in Rio de Janeiro on the afternoon of 15 May 2016.

[14] Bituca (Edgar Nunes Rocca), (Rio de Janeiro 1930-1996) was the first drummer to do field research and compile Brazilian rhythms both in their original form and adapted for drums between the 1950-60s. Here the figure was rewritten in the notation program Sibelius changing if the popular beat formula 2/4 for alla breve, 2/2, or C cut, for better graphic visualization.

Figure 3: Slow Crying.[15]

One of the factors that converge in all the statements is that the expansion of the music publishing industry has catapulted to the polkas,[16] waltzes, mazurka and xotes. This "new" media of the 19th century, the printed score, facilitated the spread of a fad that would take over not only the societies of Brazil but of all the Americas. Each place in the new continent added its local "cultural syncretism" to this phenomenon.

> **André Cardoso:** "The music publishing business was an important business because music couldn't be practiced if they didn't have the scores".

> **Henrique Cazes:** "The most important thing that happened in popular music, not only in Brazil, but all over the planet, in the second half of the 19th century, was the spread of polka in the world".

About the origin of samba, musicologist Flávio Silva diverges in his research: *Origin of Samba in Rio de Janeiro*

> **Flávio Silva: "It** was definitely not the same as the "semba" in Africa, but it had many instruments in common and a great influence of the Yoruba who were trafficked to Bahia and then came to Rio de Janeiro".[17]
> "More middle class genres: waltzes, xotes, mazurka and polkas, all these things like that... so you have a total and brutal confluence of imported European genres in the 19th century that will really make possible the constitution of what would come to be the cry... that came in scores".

> **Henrique Cazes:** "And there are two factors that will push this spread of the polka in Rio de Janeiro, one factor was the newly created music publishing industry, so it's an important factor that will have those who profit from the process of releasing those scores. And the second factor is that in Rio de Janeiro it was a city full of pianos, although the first only arrived in 1808 soon after, in 1856, Araújo Porto Alegre already called the city A Cidade dos Pianos, or Pianópolis".

---

[15] Bituca (Edgar Nunes Rocca) - Slow Cry.

[16] Polka: a lively dance of couples in 2/4 rhythm, of Bohemian origin, became one of the most popular ballroom dances of the 19th century. The music, usually in ternary form, employed characteristic rhythms, emphasizing the third eighth note of the bar. *Strauss* and other important composers of dance music wrote polkas and can be found several in *Smetana*'s music. Examples from the 20th century include *Schwanda* the *Weinberger*, Façade, *Walton*, and *Stravinsky's* Circus Polka - Groove Dictionary of Music - concise edition (1994) - Jorge Zahar Editor - p.732.

[17] Interview with musicologist Flávio Silva at his residence in Rio de Janeiro on the afternoon of May 8, 2016.

The versatility of the musicians of this scenario in the 19th century was undoubtedly one of the factors that contributed to the emergence of Choro and later Samba, according to Cardoso:

> **André Cardoso:** "I would highlight this traffic that some musicians made between classical music of European tradition and popular music. José Maurício himself was a composer who left masses, a whole series of sacred works and motetos and also left modinhas. At the same time as giving lessons using the harpsichord that comes from the European indoor culture he also used the wire guitar".

Then we have the following factors: the expanded music industry, the migration of foreign musicians as well as slaves from various African ethnic groups - mainly in the American countries bathed by the Atlantic where the traffic was a prosperous business - the greater "capacity for tolerance" and mixture of the Portuguese with the natives and slaves - compared to that of the Spanish colonizers - resulting in what Henrique Cazes calls the "cultural melting pot", which transforms the polka and the like into the language of cultural syncretism of each New World locality.

> **Henrique Cazes:** "Everywhere in America and the Caribbean where the polka was taken and there were populations of black African slaves who were taken as in Cuba, Jamaica, Haiti, New Orleans... in all these places the polka suffered the process of **syncopation[18]**".
>
> **Flávio Silva:** "Ah, the samba came from Africa? I ask: isn't the samba music all tonal? The African scales, as well as the Portuguese modal scales - which the Portuguese brought and which were Gregorian - were all absorbed by the European tonal system. Of course you still have the modalisms there in the northeast etc. That seventh down, etc. and so on, but the bulk of the samba music, the commercial samba, it's all based on European harmony, European melody".

As for the rhythmic Cazes explains in more detail the process that came to customize each genre of music during the 19th century:

> **Henrique Cazes:** "It was natural that this "polka" would then receive a bit of counter-metry. That is, a bit of things outside the time of anticipation, a character of provocation of the body, which I think is the great vector that leads to put so much counter-metry inside the polka. If we compare the Cuban Danzon, the Ragtime there in New Orleans, the Beguine in Martinique, and the Maxixe, it's all very close. Because everyone is messing with the same elements, that is: adding to the polka counter elements".

---

[18] Syncope: The regular displacement of each time in a cadenced pattern always at the same value in front of or behind its normal position in the bar - Groove Dictionary of Music - concise edition (1994) - Jorge Zahar Editor - p. 868.

Flávio Silva: "Melodically I have no doubt that she is European and harmonically she has no doubt that she is also European and there is also a kind of fusion of samba and choro, because the traditional samba naturally should not have much concern for tuning or melodic construction while the chorão had to have, were already musicians of a small bourgeois elite as Tinhorão[19] points out".

At the end of the second Empire, still with Dom Pedro II (Rio de Janeiro, 2 December 1825 - Paris, 5 December 1891), and with more force since the abolition of slavery (13 May 1888), the genre Choro is becoming more established and producing more adepts in all social classes. Many times being a crying musician could result in the cultural and financial rise of recently freed former slaves. That's why the genres that will originate the samba - maxixes, high parties and all their variations that were played in candomblé houses (Casas das Tias) - are walking parallel, "flirting" with Choro and often by the same hands as the chorões, but still in different environments.

Flávio Silva: "As Pixinguinha used to say: the choro was made in the drawing room and the samba in the backyard".

After all, does samba really come from Africa? Would the African semba be the same thing? Flávio Silva says that Samba is not African but a musical manifestation that mainly the descendants of Yoruba Africans have been building in Brazil and mixing with the culture here for a long time. On this aspect he continues:

Flávio Silva: "The samba is said to come from semba, umbigada, the traditional semba. I myself have heard hundreds of recordings of African tribal music, hundreds. I have here with me on this computer (in his residence) hundreds of recordings of records made in Africa in the 1950s, in tribes like this, and even in cities, when I had not yet had the invasion of American music, the invasion of jazz or Caribbean music in Africa and I NEVER heard anything like samba in any tribal music. So this story that samba came from Africa is a fallacy. You even have in São Paulo the samba rural paulista that Mário de Andrade described in a fantastic article, and I saw some time ago a set of these: the samba rural paulista is a semi-indigenous business where a row of men and a row of women - the men playing their instruments - and the rows are getting closer, then each man gave each woman an umbilada and then everyone went back to their places and continued in this accordioned experience: row goes and row comes. It was not samba in a circle".

---

[19] José Ramos Tinhorão (Santos, 1928) Brazilian journalist, music critic and music researcher wrote among others: Música Popular, Música Popular no Romance Brasileiro (3 volumes), Os Sons Que Vem da Rua, Os Sons dos Negros no Brasil, Os Negros em Portugal: uma presença silosa (1988), Fado: dança do Brasil cantar de Lisboa o fim de um mito (1994), etc. There have been more than 15 books on the subject of Brazilian popular music.

About the choro, and the explanation of its appearance, Maestro André Cardoso highlights some names that came to form the popular instrumental music in Rio de Janeiro. Then Cazes lists the great musicians of the first generations of choro still in the 19th century.

> **André Cardoso:** "You also have (in the 19th century) Joaquim Calado who had a training as a classical flutist, student of the conservatory of music and then became a teacher of the conservatory of music, and who was a fundamental musician for the establishment of popular music, instrumental music, choro".
>
> **Henrique Cazes:** "And a group of composers appears right at the beginning that we can quote here: Joaquim Calado, Chiquinha Gonzaga, Ernesto Nazaré and Anacleto de Medeiros".
>
> **André Cardoso:** "...many of them come from the music band (military bands): Anacleto de Medeiros for example, who was the founder and conductor of the fire service band".

The formation of a military band is essential for the first instrumental orchestrations in Brazilian popular music of that time. The first and most famous was the Fire Brigade Band that exists to this day, with Anacleto de Medeiros as its patron. Professor André "Boxexa" Santos points out about this formation:

> **Professor André "Boxexa" Santos:** "And a lot of that comes from the music band. There you play polkas, mazurcas, dobrados... military music can't be separated from that here in Brazil".[20]

Flávio Silva clarifies a polemic theme: was there percussion in the first Choro formations outside the military bands?

> **Flávio Silva:** "Choro has a much more basic origin in melodic instruments, instruments indeed, I mean: strings and wind. Once I commented with Canhoto, Canhoto was the cavaquinist of the legendary group Época de Ouro: Canhoto, in the old days choro didn't have a pandeiro, right? And he thought a little bit and answered: yes, there wasn't!".
> "The pandeiro in choro only became mandatory when the choro was converted into regional for recordings or to play on radios. Then it had to be. In the surveys I made of the choro groups in the newspapers from 1916 to 1918 the presence of percussion instruments is null".[21]
>
> **Henrique Cazes:** "This all happens in the 19th century and these musicians establish a pattern of composition that is followed by the people of their generation and the

---

[20] Interview with Prof. André "Boxexa" Santos on the afternoon of May 5, 2016 in the studios of the Pocket Orchestra in Rio de Janeiro.

[21] E-mail sent to me on May 7, 2017 Flavio Silva corrects: "My statement that the presence of percussion instruments in the choro groups is null has to be corrected. I was relying on a wrong memory. Reviewing now the information brought by the press in the period 1916-18, he gives much more prominence to wind instruments and strings than to percussions, but they are also cited, only in much lesser prominence. Even photos of choro groups attest to the predominance of so-called melodic instruments over percussion. But it is possible, yes, to say that percussion at that time was not compulsory in choro groups".

younger generation. In what way does this music spread? It spreads through some vectors, one of them is the Band of Music, the Anacleto de Medeiros already was musicalized by a guy that already had contact with the choro and he will musicalize I don't know how many people in the bands that he was directing, hundreds that are learning already inside that language, inside that accent. Ernesto Nazaré will be demonstrating the scores in the shops, he will be inside that circuit and Chiquinha Gonzaga will be playing choro in the theatre. They take this music mixing professionals and amateurs for everything that is part of and even outside Rio de Janeiro, to São Paulo, to Porto Alegre...".

"... it is a music that created a very specific and strong culture and that participated, this nucleus, and particularly the nucleus linked to the Pixinguinha, to the visitors of the houses of the Tias Baianas, of the Square Eleven, participated in what was considered the foundation of the samba".

The scenery in the plain of the neighborhood of Estácio with the houses of the "Tias" Baianas was the most sophisticated in the black culture of the Yoruba descendants. This cultural environment was solidified in the surroundings of downtown Rio de Janeiro.

Flávio Silva: "One interesting thing is that they say that Estácio is the cradle of samba creation. Estácio was not on the hill, Estácio is on the plain".

Drummer and researcher André Tandeta comments on the first phonographic record we have of a "Samba", *Pelo Telefone*, by Donga and Mauro de Almeida, already in 1916, but which "translates" what had been done "clandestinely"[22] until then - because Samba was forbidden until that year.

André Tandeta (drummer): "There is something very interesting that is this samba - cantarola: "The Chief of Police (Over the Phone)", and several others... are actually

Maxixes. Samba as we interpret, that business of semicolcheias, that came from Estácio: Ismael Silva, Bide, Armando Marçal - Marçalzinho's grandfather and mestre Marçal's father - and author and composer and partner of Bide. They were the guys from the drums. The drums were already the heart of the "business". I keep hearing that in the samba type of Donga or João da Baiana there was a little percussion that didn't have much importance there, it was more of a "groovezinho", a little rhythm, all in the diminutive itself. These guys who introduced a more present rhythm, came out a little from "Corta-jaca" (Maxixe)".[23]

Flávio Silva: "The Ishmael and Bide who were from the hill, but they went to join is in the plain, in Estácio. All right, Francisco Alves went up the hill to buy samba in all that "commerce", a fantastic story that I think is incredible. But to say that the samba came from the hill".

"And there is something else, the blacks who came from Bahia and who were a high Yoruba lineage: Tia Ciata and Hilário Jovino were a kind of African nobility. They

---

[22] E-mail sent to me on May 7, 2017 Flavio Silva points out that: "the statement by drummer André Tandeta that "samba was forbidden until that year [1916]" would need to be more contextualized. The persecution there was not against a genre that did not exist - Samba - but against festivities called Samba, that is, parties".

[23] Interview with drummer André Tandeta on the afternoon of 13 June 2016 in the studios of the Pocket Orchestra in Rio de Janeiro.

were blacks of high culture. These people who came from Bahia and brought these parades that were practiced in Bahia, and who settled a lot in candomblé houses at the time there of Praça Onze in the house of Tia Ciata, Tia Siciliane, Tia Sabata, Tia Isso and Tia Aquilo, these people were a kind of black and a kind of culture... And outside of that they had all the huge wave of former slaves or children of slaves who left the valley of the river Paraíba who were Bantu blacks, not Yoruba blacks. These Bantu had a very different culture from the Yoruba blacks. They were much more pros morros than the blacks who came from Bahia. Pixinguinha was an elite musician, you know?"

Cazes emenda sobre o ícone da música brasileira, o saxofonista e compositor Alfredo da Rocha Vianna Filho, o Pixinguinha:

Henrique Cazes: "With that maxixe accent from the class of Praça Onze lá do Pixinguinha. Pixinguinha will be there, that is to say: the greater genius of crying will be participating directly in the structuring".

Reflecting on the first statement here transcribed by the renowned drummer Wilson das Neves that *"Everything is Samba"* we can place another, by Maestro André Cardoso on the multiplicity of genres in Brazil.

Maestro André Cardoso: "Obviously Brazilian music is much richer and it's not just Samba, Choro and Bossa-Nova. Perhaps the richest diversity on the planet. The explanation for this phenomenon is clear from these statements above and is related to the mixes that the Americas underwent, enhanced here by the unique phenomenon of the Brazilian colony becoming the seat of the kingdom of Portugal between 1808 and 1821 and then having two emperors, Dom Pedro I and Dom Pedro II, all between 1808 and 1889. In those 81 years Brazil stood out and planted excellence in the creation of its musical identity".

2. PIXINGUINHA - FIRST LINES OF BASS[24]

From the first chorões appears a genius descendant of the Yoruba,[25]coming from the neighborhood of Catumbi and frequenter of the houses of the Aunts in Praça Onze, Alfredo da Rocha Vianna Filho, the Pixinguinha (Rio de Janeiro, 1897-1973).

Musician[26] (composer, flutist and saxophonist), son of musicians and brother of musicians, he was the great artist of his time and of the decades that would still come. It was the biggest of the references for Radamés Gnatalli. Both passed from live music in the confectioneries and cinemas of Rio de Janeiro to the recordings (Pixinguinha still took the mechanical recordings and then both participated in the then modern electrical recordings), to the radios and finally to the rest of the world in a few decades.

> **Flávio Silva:** "Pixinguinha was an elite musician, you know? If you go for "Carinhoso", the construction of "Carinhoso" you can even compare with the 5th Beethoven Symphony. The incised and very small and that he goes developing".

> **Luís Filipe de Lima (guitarist and writer):** "Well, some people have[27] said that to sum up the whole history of Brazilian music one word is enough: Pixinguinha".[28]

About the opportunities of work and social ascension by the music market seen by the poorer classes at the end of the 19th century, the drummer André Tandeta speaks:

> **André Tandeta (drummer and teacher):** "The job market that emerged and that in a certain way stimulated those who wanted to study music for real, because at that time when music was spoken of, it was basically orchestras, small or big orchestras, but they were orchestras".

---

[24] This chapter of the documentary can be seen at: < https://www.youtube.com/watch?v=m6E3Vf0zzZw&feature=youtu.be>.

[25] According to the musicologist Flavio Silva on page 19 of this dissertation.

[26] Alfredo da Rocha Vianna Filho was born in the Piedade district of Rio de Janeiro on 23 April 1897, the son of Alfredo da Rocha Vianna and Raimunda Maria da Conceição. His father, a post office employee, was also an amateur flutist and held musical meetings in his home, which were attended by renowned criers of the time. The boy would have received from his African grandmother or a cousin called Eurydice the nickname Pizindim (whose meaning would be "good boy"). Some believe that the name Pixinguinha is derived from the mixture of this nickname with "Bexiguinha", because as a child he had his face marked by smallpox (popularly called bladder). As a boy, he was initiated in the cavaquinho by his brothers Léo and Henrique. In a short time, he began to accompany his father to the dances. Around 1908, Pixinguinha composed his first song, the choro Lata de leite. His first music teacher was César Borges Leitão, his father's coworker, but his improvement in flute came through Irineu Batina, at the time director of harmony of the carnival ranch Filhas da Jardineira. In the ranch orchestra, Pixinguinha met two friends who would accompany him to the end of his life: João Machado Guedes, the João da Bahiana, and Ernesto dos Santos, the Donga. - Quote from the IMS website at: http://www.ims.com.br/ims/explore/artista/pixinguinha/sobre-pixinguinha.

[27] E-mail sent to me on May 7, 2017 Flávio Silva points out: *"Ary Vasconcelos (Rio de Janeiro, 1926 - 2003) was the one who said that Brazilian popular music was just a word.*

[28] Interview filmed with guitarist and writer Luís Filipe de Lima on 12 December 2016 at the Botanical Garden, Rio de Janeiro.

Henrique Cazes (cavaquinist and teacher): "Then the regional[29] will offer guitarists and cavaquinists, and then also popular percussionists, the first job opportunities. That will make all the difference. In an instrument like the cavaquinho, if I hadn't had that opportunity we would be here more or less like the cavaquinho is there in Portugal".

Luís Filipe de Lima: "And the history of Pixinguinha is also clear and confuses both the history of choro and the history of samba and the history of the carnival march, three genres that were born in Rio de Janeiro. A figure like that of Pixinguinha had lessons in harmony and orchestration with teacher Paulo Silva[30]. Once Paulo Silva gave an interview in which he said: look at Pixinguinha is a figure that impresses me, because when he was my student everything I told him not to do he did, but it worked".

The recordings and scores made in Brazil that we can find in the late 1910s and 1920s[31] reveal to us that the word **Samba** was used "at random" to boost sales of these products, not only in Rio de Janeiro, but from north to south, and that the genre could be found all over Brazil. Flávio Silva gives us examples of this:

Flávio Silva: "And Vicente Salles, a researcher who died recently, a fantastic figure from Pará, found a carnival samba in Belém (do Pará) in 1906 (ERRATA)[32]. A very fine score by Étori Bosel's publisher, an Italian".

Henrique Cazes: "It is impressive the recordings of a group of weepers from Porto Alegre, the Terror of the Factions, of 1913".

Flávio Silva: "Casa Electra, Electra record label from Porto Alegre, which began recording in 1913, recorded some 20 records labelled as samba between 1914 and 1916. The expression Samba Carnavalesco, which seems to have been invented by Donga - Ernesto Joaquim Maria dos Santos (Rio 1890 - 1974) - already appears on record labels before. Samba came to be designated as music of success, became synonymous with music of success. So it's not to say that samba was born as Pelo Telefone, no. First it wasn't the first recording, then it wasn't samba, it was recordings much more of maxixe than samba, right? And after the samba as we know it is only constituted even after the 1920s".

What we know as **Samba** today is far from what was recorded or edited in the 1910s. Professor André Tandeta talks about this:

André Tandeta: "They were actually maxixes".

Henrique Cazes: "This group, and particularly the group linked to Pixinguinha and connected to the people who frequent the Casas das Tias Baianas, participated in what

---

[29] Regional is the name of the formation, instrumentation, classical of the choro groups, usually counting with cavaquinho, mandolin, six-string guitar (centre guitar), seven-string guitar and wind soloist (N.A.).

[30] Paulo Silva was a renowned teacher of harmony and counterpoint at the National Institute of Music.

[31] In an e-mail sent to me on May 7, 2017, Flávio Silva adds: "This widespread use of the word samba occurs even in the 1920s; the word already appears in revised plays in 1916, gains strength in 1917 with Pelo Telefone, but it is in the following decade that it gains almost a meaning of successful music, without becoming the samba that would be constituted at the end of that decade.

[32] ERRATA: e-mail sent to me on May 7, 2017 Flávio Silva corrects: *"who The samba carnavalesco of Pará is from 1913/14; my information was wrong"*.

was considered the foundation of samba, marked by the launch of "Pelo Telefone", which becomes a success, a song that was actually a collection of choruses.

Although today we take as a landmark the recording of "Pelo Telefone", by the musician and composer Donga, and also as the beginning of the Samba genre, there were other Sambas that had much greater influence in Rio society. This milestone is more of a historical necessity than something that defines the genre in fact. The proximity of the genres Samba, Maxixe and Choro would still be accentuated until the 1930s.

> **Flávio Silva:** "with the success of "Pelo Telefone", a success, the word samba has been increasingly used. But "Pelo o Telefone" itself was an ephemeral success. In 1914 Cabocla de Caxangá, Cabocla de Caxangá do Catudo and João Pernambuco was sung in 14, 15, 16, 17 and in 18 *Cabocla* was sung more than Pelo o Telefone".

> **Henrique Cazes:** "Pelo o Telefone" is launched and from there the samba will begin, and the samba will have a very important aspect of having, from the first moment, its "barn of labour" in the field of harmony.

We can highlight the curious fact that there is no percussion in this first moment of Brazilian popular music, based mainly on the great research and surveys made by musicologist Flávio Silva in thousands of newspapers and periodicals from almost two decades of that period. This is one of the outstanding characteristics of Choro in the 1910s, there was no percussion. Even in Samba, which will "appear" in the middle of that decade, the presence of percussive instruments was almost ephemeral and this can be checked through the recordings that still exist.

> **André Tandeta:** "I keep listening, it seems to me that in the samba "like" Donga and João da Baiana had a little percussion so it didn't matter much".

> **Luís Filipe de Lima:** "percussion appeared a little later, in the studios about everything".

> **Flávio Silva:** "Percussion is very rare to mention percussion instruments".

> **Henrique Cazes:** "the cry NO percussion. The choro recordings have three formats at the beginning of the recordings in Brazil: a format with a guitar, a cavaquinho and a solo instrument, the trio. Another format with only three or four winds and no base. And a third format with a music band".

> **Flávio Silva:** "I have never seen mention of a group formed only of flute, ukulele and guitar. Each group was formed with what it had around it".

One of the vectors of the spread of these genera was the military band as already mentioned by Henrique Cazes. But besides this role the bands also introduce in the orchestration percussion instruments that will later become part of the drums from the 1930s.

> **André "Boxexa" Santos (drummer and teacher):** "I think it makes a lot of difference both in the way of playing and in the accentuation, in the dynamics, in the volume of sound used was the instrumental training. You have the original trio formed of flute, cavaquinho and guitar or other formations and in another moment you have the accordion playing and, finally, you didn't have the percussion, once again I think the great link in all this was the music band".

Another aspect of Samba was the very common variation in the 1920s used in carnival parades as ranches and street blocks - all travelling - which gave rise to what we know today as Schools of Sambas. This type of popular manifestation with parades in movement was inherited mainly from the Yoruba culture that underwent a process of syncretization to the many others that arrived in Brazil. For the growing increase of the members in these parades the musician Alcebíades Maia Barcelos (Niterói 1902 - Rio 1975), the Bide, invented the instrument that we call Deaf[33]. This instrument is a bass drum played in the weak time, the second half, bringing the effect of "pushing" the[34] participants forward.

> **Flávio Silva:** "Even the Samba School put the samba to work. They invented the Bide - Alcebíades Maia Barcelos (Niterói 1902 - Rio 1975) - which invented the Deaf, because they needed a more serious drum to accentuate the rhythm marking (in the second half) so the Bide put the Deaf there. All this was a result of the increase in the number of extras in the Samba School. In this sense the samba itself was made to stand in the same place, it was not made in parade. This was much more of the parade traditions, of the Cucumbis, Afoxés and Ranchos. The Samba School inherits all this and it will emerge a lot in a movement that is almost of emancipation or greater presence of these lower classes, let's say. In a time that the ranch parades will disappear, because the ranch parades were really middle class. The description that Jota Efegê gives of this is fantastic in the book, Ameno Resedá, the Ranch that was School. They were really orchestras! And those orchestras were basically of wind and strings, the Ranchos. So the Samba School will not only inherit the things that came from Bahia, it will also inherit a bit of a structure that comes from the Ranchos and even from the great societies that were imitations of the Venetian Carnivals. That was a creation of the sambistas who took all that and made a salad, and put the samba to walk!".

This whole scenario would hatch in the first phonographic successes of the genre. The new record labels as well as the radios that would appear soon after would take advantage of all this and consolidate the genre more and more similar to what we are used to today.

> **Henrique Cazes:** "at that moment when samba is becoming what it would be from the 1930s onwards, the great engine of popular music in Brazil, especially since the success of Carmem Miranda. The success of Carmem Miranda and spoken of by Ruy

---

[33] This statement can be heard at: < www.youtube.com/watch?v=jAbkgq2Id_k>.

[34] A curiosity: it also happened in the similar type of parade in New Orleans, United States, for the same need, to walk with the "cortege" only that there, besides the second half also in the fourth time - for being structured in bars of four times and not two, the "off-beat" or "back beat".

Castro, Carmem's biographer, was one thing! When Carmem Miranda burst, in the early 1930s, her records sold ten times the number of times that the second place sold, which was Francisco Alves. So Carmem Miranda practically resized the recording industry in Brazil. As a result of Carmem Miranda many opportunities arose: record labels, ensembles, singers who were released "to the pimps" in the 1930s. All this happened from the strengthening of samba. And the main character in the structuring of samba and in the samba recordings that take place mainly from the moment one moves from the mechanical recording process[35] to the electric recording[36]process, around 1927/28. Four international companies come to join Odeon: Brunswick, which had an ephemeral life, and three others that stay: Columbia, Parlophone and RCA Victor. So this is an opportunity! A range of opportunities arise and who is the guy who is equipped to "dress" this samba? It's Pixinguinha!".

Figure 4: Example of Mechanical Recording, 1913 (Grammophon Collection).

---

[35] Example of Mechanical Recording (Figure 4).
[36] Example of Electrical Recording (Figure 5).

Figure 5: Electrical Recording Example, 1916 (Boston Symphony Collection).

At first we have the ophicleide and the tuba in the serious counterpoints.

Flávio Silva: "you had Sousaphone in popular music, Ophicleide and Sousaphone, tuba precursor instruments, whatever..."

Henrique Cazes: "Yes, crying used the Ophicleide in the past, a kind of Ornithorrine of wind instruments. That was a vertical metal tube, a compatible mouthpiece like the trombone or corduroy and the saxophone keying, that is: a very strange thing. But it was an instrument that adapted to play like guitars and like a ukulele. It was an instrument with a minor sound, it was not a high impact instrument to play in orchestra and it was widely used. Being that the biggest of all was the teacher of Pixinguinha, the Irineu de Almeida, that has formidable recordings playing with Pixinguinha, the Pixinguinha with 13 or 14 years solando in the flute, playing a lot in the flute and he plays very well".

2.1 Low Lines

Figure 6: The Batutas, 1910 (MIS Collection).

Some counterpoint lines are already used for other more portable bass instruments, but just as the proof of the appearance of the seven-string guitar is recorded for the first time in history with Otávio Vianna, China, Pixinguinha's older brother, from 1910 (Figure 6), we can say that the bass in choro starts right here in this[37] photo below, taken in 1912! In it is the musician Bonfiglio de Oliveira on the double bass next to Pixinguinha with only 15 years old on flute, Otávio Silva on piano and Pádua Oliveira on violin, in the choperia La Concha, in Rua da Carioca. But the seven-stringed guitar will have much more records until the beginning of the orchestrations used in radios a little over a decade after that point. About the history of the seven-string guitar Luíz Filipe de Lima speaks:

---

[37] E-mail sent to me on May 7, 2017 Flavio Silva points out: "perhaps it would be worth emphasizing a little more the issue of the portability of the bass guitar, which would need a cart to be transported. The one in the photo might 'reside' in the choper!".

Figure 7: The Contrabass and Pixinguinha at age 15, 1912 (MIS). Pixinguinha in the beer house La Concha with (from left to right) Bonfiglio de Oliveira, who also played bass, Otávio Silva and Pádua Oliveira. (MIS Collection)[38].

Figure 8: Eight Batutas, April 1922 (MIS). Pixinguinha on the saxophone in a jazz club in Buenos Aires.

---

[38] Bonfiglio de Oliveira on bass next to Pixinguinha on flute, only 15 years old, Otávio Silva on piano and Pádua Oliveira on violin, in the choperia La Concha, in Rua da Carioca - MIS.

About the way the scores of Pixinguinha were presented we can say that the parts of the regional base were mostly not written. Until the 1920s there was no modern ciphering (alphabetical numerical, for example: C7, C major chord) - there was always French baroque type ciphering, but it was not known by most musicians of regional groups. Henrique Cazes quotes that "*In the arrangement grids of Pixinguinha's ensembles one can often see "the writing of a piano guide"*, as if it were an orchestra reduction that he probably used only for rehearsal, the counterpoints of wind instruments and only.

---

[39] The parallel bass chord should be the most bass chord of the string quartet, the cello's do. And so it followed for decades, the guitar with the first steel strings (mi, si, sol, ré, lá, mi) and the seventh string, a C grave, "borrowed" from a cello.

The base musicians memorized all the arrangements, an extraordinary exercise knowing that these ensembles made several different recordings in a short period of time.

> **Henrique Cazes:** "if you think the guy played that straight business like that... that he didn't do much, it would be relatively easy to get it right, but the amazing thing is that he was able with these musicians to do sophisticated things using rhythm conventions, changes of tempo, modulations, breques, breques with different sizes for each moment of the arrangement. And the guys could memorize that and learn".

When the counterpoint of the basses leaves the ophicleide and goes to the seven strings in the group of Pixinguinha - Os Oito Batutas, or as they were called in France *Les Batutas* - China[40] and later Tute[41] had to invent a way to execute them, and this way they are used in traditional crying until today.

> **Luís Filipe de Lima:** "both Tute and China, especially China, played a style of guitar called the "**Hammer Guitar**", that guitar whose notes, whose interventions are always supported in strong time - and hums: tum, tum, tum, tum, tum... making more than three eighth notes was already an extravagance! IBIDEM

Figure 9: Transcription in musical notation of what was hummed by Luiz Filipe de Lima.

Pixinguinha, despite not yet having the bass in his main group of musicians, was a great admirer of the American formations that were beginning to arrive in Brazil seeing recordings and scores in the 1910/20. The Oito Batutas, who traveled between 1922 and 23 to France and Buenos Aires through their patron Arnaldo Guinle, were almost an American "jazz combo" formation.[42]

> **André Tandeta:** "the formation they called Jazz Band, even if it was not to play jazz".

> **Flávio Silva:** "but you have the photos of the[43] Pixinguinha group in Buenos Aires in 1922 that are from an American Big Band (actually a small band)".

> **Henrique Cazes:** "Pixinguinha will actually become an arranger from the time he returns from Paris in 1922/23, and he will work in the magazine theatre. And the magazine theatre will be his instrumentation laboratory".

---

[40] Otávio Littleton da Rocha Vianna (Rio de Janeiro 1888 - 1927), China, Pixinguinha's older brother.

[41] Artur de Souza Nascimento, known as Tute (Rio de Janeiro, 1886 - 1957).

[42] Traditional jazz training that always starts with a "piano jazz trio" (piano, bass and drums) then we add three to five winds. Bigger than that would be a "jazz small ensemble" until the formation of "jazz big band" which would be: piano, double bass, guitar, five saxophones, four trombones and four trumpets.

[43] *Eight Batutas* in 1927 with Pixinguinha on the saxophone, in a Buenos Aires jazz club - MIS - Figure 8.

The controversy that there was no double bass in the maxixe, choro or samba formations, clarified here with the 1912 photo, continues to raise doubts even in the people who had contact with some of these musicians at the beginning of the century. At the beginning of the twentieth century there were undoubtedly many more ophicleidists and tubistas making a living playing the serious counterpoints in Brazilian popular music than bassists, and the reason was simple: portability, a reason already cited by musicologist Flávio Silva in this research. So, due to the rarity of evidence such as the photograph of Choperia la Concha, many still support the false inexistence of the instrument:

> **Wilson das Neves (legend of the Brazilian drums):** "he didn't even have a double bass, the tuba that made the bass![44]

In fact, great tubistas passed through the groups of Pixinguinha, including Maestro Eleazar de Carvalho (Iguatu, 1912 - São Paulo, 1996) who was later a student in the United States of the great conductor, composer, teacher and bassist Sergey Koussevitzky (Russia 1874 - USA 1951).

> **Henrique Cazes:** "Pixinguinha when he goes to do the orchestrations he will use a lot from the beginning the tuba. Even a curiosity is that one of the tubers who recorded with Pixinguinha in the 1930s was Eleazar de Carvalho (Iguatu 1912 - São Paulo 1996). Eleazar worked a lot with Pixinguinha. They were colleagues, they knew each other from the School of Music (today UFRJ), they were colleagues in some subjects and when they asked him: Pixinguinha did you graduate from the School? He said: "I passed straight, yes, but who really studied was Eleazar!".
>
> **Omar Cavalheiro (bassist and teacher):** "the bass that Pixinguinha wrote for the tuba is a great reference for us to play the bass. We can even dry some notes, some drawings and such, but it is the great reference!".[45]

Below is a bass line written in the "Tuba Style of Pixinguinha". Even if played by another instrument you should try to sound like a tuba, without bandages, very rhythmic. The fourth below or fifth above movement, so idiomatic of the tubas, is seen in these counterpoints, and will become more linear later, in the 1930s, in the writing of Radamés Gnattali[46].

---

[44] Interview filmed with drummer legend Wilson das Neves on the afternoon of 14 August 2016 in the neighborhood of Jardim Guanabara, Rio de Janeiro.

[45] Interview filmed with bassist and teacher Omar Cavalheiro on October 5, 2016 at the Botanical Garden, Rio de Janeiro.

[46] Example video on the link: https://www.youtube.com/watch?v=HOs7eW-FsYQ.

Figure 10: Pixinguinha's Tuba style bass line written by the author for the composition of the same called *Sem Dormir*, by Lipe Portinho.

Very important for this research of the lines of the bass counterpoints is to observe the progress of the instrument that will accompany the bass from the late 1920's until today, the battery. The history of the bass is totally dependent on this "cousin brother" instrument in the rhythm section.

André Tandeta: "the drums as we know them, what in English is called drum set, I don't know when it arrived here in Brazil, but... I had already heard something in the 1920s".

Oscar "Bolão" (drummer and teacher): "Perrone[47], if I am not mistaken, is from 1908, he was already playing in 1920. He played in dairy, in cinema, in... Perrone is from the time when there were no drums yet, he told me a few things: they put the box on the back of a chair, there was no box shelf. It was a very prehistoric thing indeed! He said that when the bass drum arrived there was no pedal, he said that sometimes he even kicked the bass drum, Perrone is from that time. There are some guys who are his contemporaries: a guy who I think is a wonderful drummer called Valfrido Silva[48], from Niterói, who is a damned suingueiro, a damned sambeiro! From this generation of Perrone there is SUT..."[49]

Gildásio Paiva, o Dazinho (Brazilian drumming legend): "... SUT, old Sut. He has an old film that he played and he juggles with his drumstick ...".[50]

---

[47] Luciano Perrone (Rio de Janeiro 1908 - 2001) is considered by many the father of the Brazilian drum set. One of his phrases defines well what should be the thought of every musician in Brazil in the 1930s to 1960s: *"I never bothered to imitate Gene Krupa because what interested me was the samba drumming"*.

[48] E-mail sent to me on May 7, 2017 Flavio Silva points out: *"Valfrido Silva, if I am not mistaken, is the author of "The Emperor of Samba", which has a fantastic Carmen Miranda recording.*

[49] Interview filmed as Oscar drummer "Bolão" Pelon on June 11, 2016 at the Botanical Garden, Rio de Janeiro.

[50] Interview filmed with Gildásio Paiva, o Dazinho, on 31 October 2016 in the neighborhood of Tijuca, Rio de Janeiro (in memorian, Dazinho died less than two weeks after that).

Wilson das Neves: "Sut, Sutinho..."

Oscar "Bolão": "then came Sutinho, finally, I don't know in the other states what it was like, Sut was even Paulista, he came to live in Rio, but here in Rio de Janeiro we can say that Perrone in a general way can be considered the father of the Brazilian drums, you know?"

Henrique Cazes: "Yes, the battery was already being used. Even Luciano Perrone, with whom I talked a lot about these subjects, said that he was a guy who every time an artist came here with an outside musician, a drummer, he would go there to see something new, right? Because the drum set we're talking about is an instrument that has a bumbo that gets kicked, that doesn't have a pedal... it's not that drum set that you're going to have from the 1930s and in Brazil from 1940 on.

The battery appears, among others, for two strong motivations: cost reduction and space reduction.

Oscar "Bolão": "the drums before were three instruments, they were three guys who played the bass drum, the box and the plate".

André Tandeta: "The guy had to do there what three or four of them were doing, so he adapted".

The battery used in the United States was not yet the same as the one used here. There were many variations and improvisations in its instrumental.

Oscar "Bolão": "the little brush[51] arrived here around almost 1928/29 and before it rolled a ganzá that was something I keep imagining... can you imagine the primitive ganzá the noise that that business made? With stone in it! I even got those ganzás that had stones inside, an unbearable noise!"

André Tandeta: "the lines, right? The lines that the guys played on the different instruments were being adapted for the drums, from bass to treble".

Oscar "Bolão": "has recordings with an instrument that was used a lot in the beginning: omelê (generic name of several African percussion instruments). It happened to me that I have a recording that has an omelê solo. Then I realized that what I thought was a box without a mat was an omelê that was being played".

The great revolution attributed to Luciano Perrone is the adaptation of popular Carioca genres such as Maxixe, Choro and Samba to the drums. He was a kind of "practical ethnomusicologist", because he transcribed to the drums the batucada that he heard from his percussionist friends from candomblé houses, besides having taken many of them also to play on the radios as soon as he had the opportunity. That was the "map" so that the bassists and arrangers could create their lines.

---

[51] Brush or broom, metal piassava drumstick.

Henrique Cazes: "and Luciano Perrone said that what he did was look at the guys' batucada and transfer it to the drums. He didn't invent the samba, he learned it from those guys, only that he could make several instruments there. He made the deaf box, held it with his hand, and made a tambourine. And he copied the agogo, hung the agogo on the drums too... now, João da Baiana - João Machado Guedes (Rio 1887 - 1974) - has a special importance for Luciano, and when you hear a recording of João da Baiana, he plays the pandeiro on the samba, his pandeiro is like this: tum, chi, qui, tum, chi, qui, tum... it doesn't have one and two! On his pandeiro the one and the two are the same! Luciano learned, according to him, watching those guys play and as he was a guy who had a lot of technique, he was a guy with a privileged musical intelligence, he could solve that technically on drums".

Wilson das Neves: "It is a very complicated rhythm to write! Nobody touches it the way they write!".

André "Boxexa" Santos: "if you get the original scores, in the drum line usually comes that cell of the little forefather: tá, tá, tá, tá, tá... two voices, one that would be the box with the bass drum and some plate attacks. Only when the melody has some specific punctuation that: OK, OK, OK, OK... OK, OK, OK... in other words: you can't play the lyrics! You have to know it, so I was desperate to find Bolão!".

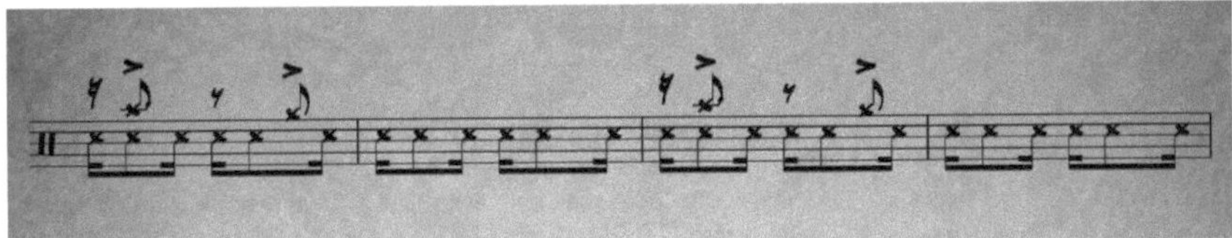

Figure 11: The "little fork" quoted by André Boxexa Santos.

As for the double bass lines that were beginning to be used at that time, Professor Omar Cavalheiro explains the need for simplicity and that we should not make the drawing much used nowadays of punctuated eighth note more semicolcheous for the counterpoint given to the compositions of this style of Choro.

Omar Gentleman: "he (Cazes) said: look, you can do anything, now, just don't do TUMTUM (punctuated eighth note plus semicolchy)! Then I started to realize that the samba sauce gets much cooler!".

Do not:

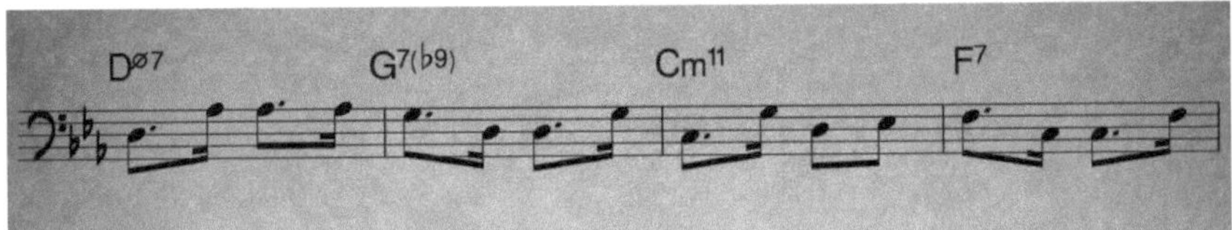

Figure 12: Not playing samba like this.

And yes do:

Figure 13: Playing samba like this.

Oscar "Predictor": "and it looks nice, you know?

Omar Cavalheiro: "two semines, you accentuate the second half and there you go in that economy... there are others doing this function, suddenly there's a rebound, something comes in, a tambourine, so in that there you do TUMTUM is congested sometimes!

To close the chapter about Pixinguinha and his style we can leave the classic formula to have bass and seven strings guitar together in the same orchestration, as Luís Filipe de Lima reminds us:

Luís Filipe de Lima: "this is a great question: what to expect from the bassist who plays along with the seven-string guitar and the seven-string guitar who plays along with the bassist? I think the question is clear to me, the bassist must hear the seven strings and the seven strings must hear the bassist. To play together is to listen".

3. RADAMÉS, THE INVENTOR OF THE FUTURE[52]

Samba Tradicional (Bituca)

♩=112

Figure 14: Bituca's Traditional Samba - 1930s to 1950s.

---

[52] This chapter of the documentary can be seen at: < https://www.youtube.com/watch?v=Nv8BG2l05Z8&feature=youtu.be>.

3.1 Radamés Gnattali & Guilherme Fontainha

Maestro André Cardoso explains the importance of another genius that comes to be part of the structuring of samba and choro and all Brazilian popular music, and that appeared through the hands of a great teacher of the National Institute of Music, today School of Music of UFRJ, teacher and maestro Guilherme Halfeld Fontainha.

André Cardoso: "Radamés had pretensions of becoming a concert performer".

Henrique Cazes: "At the first audition of Tchaikovsky's B-flat Concert in Brazil the soloist was Radamés Gnattali.

André Cardoso: "Guilherme Fontainha plays[53] a very important role in the beginning of Radamés' career. First that Fontainha played both in Rio de Janeiro and Rio Grande do Sul. There he played an important role in the development of musical education in Rio Grande do Sul, the state where Radamés Gnattali comes from. Fontainha - who is from Juiz de Fora in the state of Minas Gerais - settled in Rio de Janeiro and Radamés came to meet him shortly afterwards. Radamés intended to become a concert performer, so much so that the first concert Radamés does in Rio de Janeiro is at the Instituto Nacional de Música - now UFRJ - in the Leopoldo Miguez hall, he presents the sonata in Liszt's Sol Minor, which is an extraordinary piece, a "tour de force" for each and every pianist. Obviously Radamés' musical formation also has a strong presence in popular music and opera, he is not called Radamés for nothing - and his sister is called Aida. Of course, Fontainha had the pretension that Radamés was a concert pianist".

British bassist and composer Paul McCartney in 1994 wrote a note that was eternalized in his[54] authoritative biography by photographer Barry Miles[55]: "I feel like the sixties is about to happen, It feels like a period in the future to me, rather than a period in the past" - "I feel that the sixties are about to happen, it feels like a period in the future to me, rather than a period in the past". We can say that the "future" of the recording industry and of the genres we know today as Brazilian popular music is in the 1940s, more precisely in the '43s, in the program "Um Milhão de Melodias"[56], which took place in Rio de Janeiro, in the studios of Rádio Nacional, under the direction of the radio broadcaster from Minas Gerais, José Mauro, and arrangements by the maestro Radamés Gnattali. The arranger joined the radio in 1936 from the competitor Mayrink Veiga, in a strategy to become the number one in audience... It worked.

---

[53] Maestro Guilherme Halfeld Fontainha (Juiz de Fora 1887 - Rio 1970).

[54] *Many Years From Now* (1997) - Miles, Barry - Londres: Holt Paperbacks, 1998, p I.

[55] Barry Miles was a photographer for the Beatles throughout most of the group's rise and became one of the band leader's greatest friends and in 1997 wrote his version of Paul McCartney's biography.

[56] The repertoire to be presented in "Um Milhão de Melodias" was chosen by Paulo Tapajós and Haroldo Barbosa, directed by José Mauro.

The programme has been on the air for 13 years. It had the legendary Luciano Perrone on drums, Pedro Vidal Ramos on bass, Aníbal Augusto Sardinha, the boy, on guitar and also on this instrument Bola Sete and later Zé Menezes, on percussion João da Baiana and Heitor dos Prazeres and Radamés himself on piano.

But to try to explain the Radamés phenomenon and its innovative way of writing for regional groups we have to understand its trajectory. Gaúcho, born in 1906 in Porto Alegre, son of Italian immigrants Adélia Fossati Gnattali, a piano teacher, and Alessandro Gnattali, a bassist, bassoonist and conductor. He was fortunate to be a student of one of the founders of most music schools in the southeast and south of Brazil, Maestro Guilherme Fontainha[57]. Between 1904 and 1914 Fontainha studied in Berlin and Paris, where he was the disciple of one of Franz Liszt's last students, pianist Conrad Ansorg, and then he was the pupil of Michael von Zadora, disciple of Busoni. Fontainha brought Radamés to Rio for the first time in 1923 and then again at the end of the 1920s, this time to stay and try a teacher's competition at the former National Institute of Music, now the UFRJ School of Music. Then came the revolution of 1930...

> **André Cardoso (conductor and teacher):** "Radamés himself in a statement explains that the revolution of the 1930s was a milestone in his career, that he hoped to enter the National Institute of Music as a teacher through a competition and that the revolution of the 1930s postponed the competition for which he was preparing and he ended up going into pianistic practice in silent cinemas, in cafes and on the radios, first at Mayrink Veiga and then at Nacional. Where he built his career. He was fundamental in the Brazilian music of the 20th century and in a certain way the compositional work of Radamés transits in the tradition of European music with symphonies, quartets and sonatas and everything else, but with the strong presence of the language of popular music and jazz, of what he had as a musical practice on the radio".

Radio, especially the two leaders in the 1940s, Rádio Mayrink Veiga and Nacional, were the cultural source of Brazil, explains bassist Luiz Alves, one of the musicians who participated actively in music from the 1950s on, played in the famous nightclubs of post six in

---

[57] Guilherme FONTAINHA (management 1931-1937), Guilherme Halfed Fontainha was born in Juiz de Fora (MG) on 25 June 1887. He studied piano at the National Institute of Music. He moved to Europe where he perfected himself in Berlin and Paris. He performed in recitals in Berlin, Turin and Lisbon before returning to Brazil. In 1916 he went to live in Porto Alegre, where he directed the Conservatory of Music and founded the Society of Artistic Culture. In Rio Grande do Sul he founded conservatories in different municipalities such as Pelotas, Rio Grande and Bagé. He returned to Rio de Janeiro, where he became a teacher at the National Institute of Music and, in 1931, was named its director. Among his actions is the creation of the Revista Brasileira de Música, the first journal of musicology in the country. He wrote and published "O Ensino do piano" (1956) and "A criança e o piano" (1968). He died in Rio de Janeiro in 1970. - source: UFRJ Music School website at: http://www.musica.ufrj.br/index.php?option=com_content&view=article&id=132&Itemid=152.

Copacabana and then became part of movements such as Bossa-Nova and later Brazilian Popular Music of the 1970s, which we will see in the next chapter.

> **Luiz Alves (bassist):** "The formation we had was more by radio, the television started later and there was nothing of music. There was the Rádio Nacional orchestra with Chiquinho do Acordeom, it was the biggest culture of the time and where we learned something. Ah, the Radamés, of course! The Radamés quintet that was the basis of things".[58]

> **Biju, (Moacyr Viana Marques da Silva (saxophonist):** "Radamés was the conductor of Rádio Nacional, I worked with him at Rádio, I had an orchestra with five saxophones, I had a regional ensemble, Rádio Nacional had everything![59]

The development of radios in Brazil cost a little to happen, there were experiences before the 1930s, but it was only in the mid-30s and early 40s that radio became popular, explains musicologist Flávio Silva:

> **Flávio Silva:** "There is a border! So much so that the great development of the radio the great popularization of the radio will happen not at the time that the guy took a bamboo and stretched a wire and took the one of the "galena radio" to listen to radio with a infernal squeak, but it will happen from the moment that the radio gets electrified and that the record gets electrified, at the same time".

Radamés Gnattali will take a ride on the success of the radios already as an arranger, a more important post than that of just an instrumental pianist.

> **Henrique Cazes:** "from 1936 Radamés, who was a pianist in RCA Victor, also began to write his arrangements. And just as Pixinguinha had Carmen Miranda to succeed with the song "Taí" and spread his name as an arranger, Radamés had Orlando Silva, the singer of the crowds, and Radamés then became, with a very different characteristic from Pixinguinha, an orchestrator. He used strings and when we speak strings many times in those recordings of the 40's he was a cello and two violins. It was a very small thing... the studios were small and the technical conditions were also small, but he did that with a lot of whim, for example the song "Lábios que Eu Beijei" which has the first cello solo of popular music in Brazil, sung by Orlando Silva, with Iberê Gomes Grosso on cello. These are remarkable things that will make Radamés stand out from Pixinguinha and they will distribute the repertoire on the label, Radamés taking care of the most romantic part and Pixinguinha the most carnival part, the marchinhas, etc.".

> **Flávio Silva:** "I once heard Humberto Franceschi[60], a tremendous collector of recordings, a guy much more radical than Tinhorão in matters of fidelity to his origins.

---

[58] Interview filmed as bassist Luiz Alves on April 18, 2016 in Copacabana, Rio de Janeiro.

[59] Interview filmed with musician Moacyr Viana Marques da Silva, the Biju, on April 13, 2016 in the neighborhood of Grajaú, Rio de Janeiro.

[60] Humberto Franceschi (Rio de Janeiro 1930-2014) was a writer, researcher, collector and photographer. He is considered one of the greatest authorities in the field of sound technology. For decades, he has divided himself between research on the history of the Brazilian recording industry - which resulted in two essential books - and the search for 78-rpm records. The collection, which began as a hobby, eventually became one of the country's

He once showed me some arrangements by Radamés that were cheap imitations of American things. But it was that business, Radamés had to manufacture instrumentation one after the other. From time to time he had time and more interest in music to do something better. But when he had to do something he would write anyway".

Everything needed to be invented or reinvented, the way of playing the samba in the groups that were being regimented, true *jazz bands,* with drums, piano and double bass, was new here, but it was a copy of the format that for more than a decade had worked in the United States. We are in an era, 1930s, where drummers appear playing foreign rhythms (foxtrot and ragtime) without knowing exactly how to "translate" what was already being heard in the regionals and the bassists were beginning to deal with songs almost all without the bow and having to start reading ciphered chords instead of traditional musical notation. Radamés invented the future, from it there was a written and recorded base to be studied and copied by others in various formations. He even innovated by "deconstructing" what was already sedimented, as when he "corrupted" what was done to the bass counterpoints on the seven-string guitar, something that he could take to the extreme later in the Camerata Carioca in[61]the 1970s and 1980s.

Luís Filipe de Lima: "the seven-stringed phrases he wrote... the seven-stringed guitar is a kind of "continuous bass" of choro and samba, it is played in a free and improvised way and of course has its space delimited and a delimited language as well as a delimited phraseology, but within a lot of space. Very few people wrote sentences for the seven-string guitar, at most obligations - what is called more in the electric guitar vocabulary of riffs. But apart from that it was very rare for someone to write an arrangement with phrases from end to end for the seven-string guitar. Even a musician who saw a score in front of him would "slap" the arranger. Now, in that context he wrote for the Camerata Carioca, with arrangements that valued nuances and each instrument solvated, the cavaquinho was able to solar certain stretches and also make contracantos not only accompaniments and the guitars ídem in that formation. Then Radamés began to write phrases that also did not have much of the face of the traditional seven-string guitar, they already had other elements, harmonizations that were not common to traditional choro and some phrases with clearly pianistic meaning. Of course. It was not for nothing, Radamés knew fully what he was doing".

---

greatest sound collections, with recordings covering the entire first half of the 20th century. Source: Instituto Moreira Salles.

[61] The original Camerata Carioca was: Joel do Nascimento (mandolin), Raphael Rabello (seven-string guitar), Luciana Rabello (ukulele), Maurício Carrilho (six-string guitar), Celsinho Silva (tambourine) and Luiz Otávio Braga (six-string guitar).

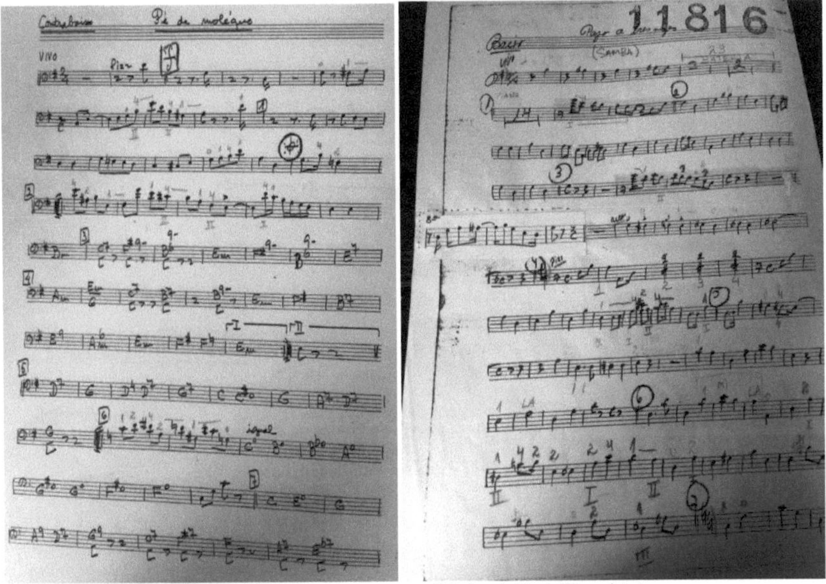

Figure 15: Original bass scores of Radamés Gnatalli's quintet.

Radamés was the son of a bassist (also a bassoonist and conductor), for this reason he mastered the writing for the instrument, he always knew how to explore the serious counterpoint and adapted the genres for the instrument from the first moment, always giving the musician freedom to express himself.

> **Omar Cavalheiro (bassist and teacher):** "Radamés sometimes did the whole part, in "Chatting Three Voices" he did everything! If you look at the score it is black with notes, the original score that the bassist Pedro Vidal Ramos played. I made one or two modifications when we re-recorded it with the New Quintet, but there was a lot of **cipher** hour, hour the bass **line written** (notation), so he also gave freedom, he had a characteristic that what the musician did on top of what he wrote he gave "carte blanche", he approved! He used to say it like this: "gee, I wrote the arrangement, but you're playing! It's the double bass! Do it!".

3.2 Alphabetic Numerical Encryption

Many musicians maintain the "impression" that there were no chord encoding in the 30s, 40s and 50s, because Radamés was just one of the exceptions to using that language. The numerical alphabetic ciphering of the chords, or American ciphering, as it was known, appears more strongly in the pre-Bossa-Nova moment, but it was already used since 1940, just check the material of Radamés Gnattali's quintet.

The musician Zeca Assumpção, who replaced the pioneer bassist Pedro Vidal Ramos, undoes that impression, with the excellence of those who played with Radamés with the same material that was used since the radio era.

About the appearance of the chords ciphered as a language and how difficult it was to have access to that information speaks the musician Henrique Cazes:

An important figure in the aspect of chord making in Brazil was Aníbal Augusto Sardinha, the Boy[63], a multi-instrumentalist who was a great experimenter in the field of chords

---

[62] Interview filmed with bassist Zeca Assumpção on October 2, 2016 at the Jardim Botânico, Rio de Janeiro.

[63] Aníbal Augusto Sardinha, the Boy (São Paulo 1915 - Rio de Janeiro 1955) was a Brazilian composer, guitarist and multi-instrumentist. Son of Portuguese immigrant couple Antônio Augusto Sardinha and Adosinda dos Anjos Sardinha, he was the first born in Brazil. His father played Portuguese guitar and guitar. Since very early he became interested in music, starting his experiments in an improvised wooden and string guitar. From the age of 11, he began to work to help support the house, employing himself as a helper in an instrument shop located in the neighborhood of Brás. His first instrument, a banjo, was given to him by his brother Batista, who in addition to strumming the instrument, was a guitarist and singer. Throughout his career, he studied music with Atílio Bernardini and composition with João Sepe, studying related subjects with Radamés Gnattali, of whom he was a great friend. In 1926, at the age of 11, he began playing Banjo in the Armani Brothers Regional ensemble, becoming known since then as Moleque do Banjo. His first opportunity came in 1929, when, in the exhibition at the Palace of Industries, he performed in a large ensemble playing alongside Canhoto, Zezinho and Mota. Later, they formed an orchestral ensemble. His entry into artistic life was initially due to the singer Paraguassu, with whom he made his first recordings and several excursions through the interior of São Paulo. In 1930, he made his solo record debut, when Maestro Francisco Mignone, at the time artistic director of Parlophon, received him for a test, alongside the guitarist Serelepe. They were invited to record on the same day, recording the maxixe-choro "Bichinho de queijo" and the maxixe "Driblando," both compositions by him, in a duo of banjo and guitar. Performing at the Quarta Caravana Artística and at Rádio Clube Paranaense, he received a proposal to   perform with Aimoré at the Farroupilha Casino, in Porto Alegre, where they signed their first contract as a duo. From there they went to Argentina, following Carlos Gardel in some numbers. Returning to São Paulo, the duo introduced themselves to Sílvio Caldas, who invited them to a season in Santos, where they achieved great success playing tenor guitar. In 1936, he recorded with hawaiian guitar solos with Aimoré's accompaniment two of his works, the choro "Dolente" and the waltz "Moreninha". In this same year, by indication of Sílvio Caldas and through César Ladeira, Garoto and Aimoré were invited to play in Mayrink Veiga Radio, a broadcaster that had at the time one

still in the 1930's and belonged to Radamés Gnattali's ensemble. Boy traveled with Carmem Miranda to the United States, where he could have learned the numerical alphabetic cipher used there, according to professor Paulo Sá.

> **Paulo Sá (teacher and mandolinist):** "The importance of the Boy (Aníbal Augusto Sardinha): he was born in 1915 (São Paulo) and died in 1955 (Rio de Janeiro), he had a very short life and with 25 years he was already a professional musician, a musician made practically, he had a lightning trajectory, he was already famous in the musical environment of São Paulo, from there the nickname "Boy", because since very early he already stood out. The invitation of Carmen Miranda was as he came to Rio de Janeiro, for the musical wheels, and it was soon known. He played not only the guitar, but other instruments like the tenor banjo, initially his nickname was "Garoto do Banjo". He already had a great resourcefulness on the guitar and used some bold harmonies, he did that naturally. Carmem Miranda called him to the Banjo da Lua[64], in 1939 he was already in the United States and in 1940 he had, back in Brazil, contact with Radamés Gnattali and in 1946 he went to Radio. The importance of him in the harmonic field, in my opinion, was that he had an in loco contact with the American jazz culture, while he was there many of those jazz musicians, Thelonious Monk, Dizzy Gillespie, all those went to see the Moon Gang playing not for Carmem Miranda, but to listen to the Boy. So obviously he had there the direct contact with this harmonic part of the jazz and naturally he brought this in his musical baggage, we can call it influence, for Brazil".[65]

The difficulty in learning chord ciphering even in the 1950s is exemplified by the most successful Bossa Nova producer, Roberto Menescal. Menescal is a guitarist and arranger and was a student of Guerra-Peixe, among others.

> **Roberto Menescal (producer and guitarist):** "I remember the first thing like this (cipher) was with Carlinhos Lyra, I was about 18 years old, I had one year of guitar, and I went to school at night because of the army, and on the first day of the army they already talked to me like this: there is a guy here who plays guitar and is a composer and even has a recorded song, imagine! It was Carlinhos Lyra who had recorded a song of his with (singer) Sylvinha Telles. So they took me to him and I said: how cool do you play? So let's go home and play! So we already "killed" the first day of class and I ended up "killing" the whole year, at the end of the year I stopped, because I saw that I couldn't study. But Carlinhos already wrote a cipher, half of him, she knew a little something, she learned I don't know if with the boy, because he became friends with the boy. I also remember that they spoke to me of a guitarist called Bandeirante[66] who lived in the neighborhood of Botafogo and that had a method of chords. I took a bus I went to Botafogo, in a small village, and he sold the method, I bought, it was a method of chords that said more or less like this: I, II, III of the tone and passage, passage was chord of the first degree with seventh. It was this in the various shades, but it was not yet spoken in a cipher, it spoke, for example: C, Sun with the seventh, the maximum of the cipher was this... passage, which was the tonic with the seventh

---

of the best cast in Rio. Quote: Dicionário Cravo Albin da Música Popular Brasileira, in the link: http://dicionariompb.com.br/garoto.

[64] Bando da Lua was the group that accompanied the singer Carmem Miranda in Brazil and the United States, several musicians stood out there and some became great producers, as the case of Aloysio de Oliveira that we will see in the next chapter.

[65] Interview filmed with Professor Paulo Loureiro de Sá on April 4, 2017 in Rio de Janeiro.

[66] Bandeirante (São Paulo 1923- Rio de Janeiro 1980) was called Edhir Izzi Lins and taught harmony classes in the years 1940-50 and had an edited method: more information at: http://www.violaobrasileiro.com.br/dicionario/visualizar/Bandeirante-Edhir-Izzi-Lins.

(to go to the neighbouring tone). I walked around in everything and started to make my cipher and when it had a slightly different chord I wrote it is X with the note in reverse, C7 with the note in reverse, for example, which is C7(9) - or only C9 in the American cipher. And so I went on doing, but then another musician started to discover something, and when I assembled my quintet that had Sérgio Barrozo (double bass), Hugo Marotta (vibraphone), etc. Hugo and Sérgio brought a little cipher (as they understood it) and we were unifying the cipher, OUR cipher. Until today I don't know what is right. I write some things in a way here comes the guy... Andy Summers comes from England, guitarist of "the Police" and asks: "this chord of seventh major that you are talking is this: C△ ? And he draws a "little pyramid" that's a way of writing, I don't know what's right! We started to get the scores, ask for scores from outside, and there we started to see the form they used most. I won't tell you if it's right or wrong that I wouldn't know, but it was the way the orchestras used there, so in 1957-58 we started to have a conscience that there was a language to facilitate even, instead of writing everything".[67]

Henrique Cazes: "I believe that for a moment in the early 1940s this figure appeared, which was a simplification that greatly improved the lives of people who wrote a lot. Radamés said: "When it was short of time I would put a cipher up and write SOLO DE PIANO, I would do it on time", there was no time to make the arrangement".

Luiz Alves (bassist): "But I really started to study independently (self-taught), more playing. In recordings with Wagner Tyso (pianist), we started playing together, at that time we were young, and we played in several formations and I kept getting things like that".

From this scenario we can then conclude that between the end of the 1930s and the 1950s the bassists who then appeared to meet the demand for radios had to fit into this new ciphered language, in addition to having knowledge of traditional notation, still widely used. Yes, there were bass in many recordings already, the 1950s were very good, marketing-wise, for this instrument and for the jazz piano trios (piano, bass and drums) to the detriment of the regional ones. The seven-string guitar was losing space for the new bassists. Radamés wrote for the instrument very early on and was, perhaps unwittingly, one of the main vectors of its popularization.

3.3 Double bass and the battery "hand in hand" in the new language

Henrique Cazes: "Radamés is going to use bass very early, he even has that play dedicated to his father: "Song and Dance", it was a play from the times of youth dedicated to his father. A piece that has already been played, I myself saw Sandrino (Santoro) playing it".

Radamés' main bassist was Pedro Vidal Ramos, a gaucho born at the beginning of the 20th century who studied bass with the Italian Rodolfo Battesine in Uruguay and returned to

---

Brazil in the late 1920s. The musician played both in classical music - he was the main bassist of the National Symphony Orchestra - and in popular music. Vidal, as he was known, is still a reference today for us to identify the style of playing bass throughout the Radio Age in Brazil, from 1930 to 1950. He was as legendary as he was enigmatic for the history of Brazilian music, as the lack of information about his personal life is curious, as well as his disappearance in the mid-1980s after having thousands of records in phonograms.

> **Sandrino Santoro (bassist and teacher):** "Vidal (Pedro Vidal Ramos), who was a great friend of mine, and we played together at the National Symphony Orchestra one next to the other, one does he was spalla after me, so it was a wonderful thing![68]
>
> **Dazinho - Gildásio Paiva (drummer):** "Vidal had a craze to talk difficult!
>
> **Sandrino Santoro:** "He was a student in Uruguay at (Rodolfo) Battesine. We got along very well.

Sandrino Santoro, when asked about the whereabouts of his colleague from the National Symphony Orchestra, simply couldn't answer what his end was, as well as all the other twenty interviewed in this survey. Vidal disappeared in the mid 1980s. The oldest musicians remember him even without being able to say his whereabouts.

> **André Tandeta (drummer and teacher):** "Vidal was from the Radamés group and the musicians "from the old days" have many stories with Vidal, some very funny".
>
> **Oscar "Bolão" Pelon (drummer):** "I don't know, but I think it's something from the forties, the group was: Vidal (double bass), Chiquinho do Acordeom (on the accordion), before Zé menezes (guitar) was the Boy, Luciano Perrone (drums) and Radamés (piano)".

Henrique talks about the modernity of the arrangements of Radamés and his group, with Pedro Vidal Ramos and Luciano Perrone still in the 1940s.

> **Henrique Cazes:** "an example that we can look for from a standard orchestration as it is today is the original recording of the song "Copacabana[69]" (1946 by Braguinha and Alberto Ribeiro released by Continental) with Dick Farney singing and strings, a very beautiful arrangement, beautiful harmony, and there is the bass and double bass is Vidal, Pedro Vidal Ramos, who was a Radamés partner already there in Rádio Nacional, before they would certainly have played in some places and had something:

---

[68] Interview filmed with Professor Sandrino Santoro on April 7, 2016 in the Flamengo neighborhood of Rio de Janeiro.

[69] The song *Copacabana* by João de Barro and Alberto Ribeiro can be heard on the link: < https://www.youtube.com/watch?v=s9c614gBu6U >.

Luciano Perrone met Radamés in 1929 and they went to work together from 1929 until 1986 when Radamés got sick".

André Tandeta: "They met Radamés and Perrone in Poços de Caldas - MG - playing in a casino".

About Luciano Perrone, revolutionary drummer of the Radamés groups, speaks Wilson das Neves.

Wilson Das Neves: "He was a soloist, a drummer. There are some who are and some who are not. I never worried about manning, for example, I'd sunbathe four bars, eight at most, and I was already finding a lot, because my business was to accompany the orchestra in my own way".

The bassist Pedro Vidal Ramos was replaced when he "retired" by Zeca Assumpção, from São Paulo, in the 1980s. Zeca was back in Brazil after studying in the United States and was assimilated by Radamés, who was always a great enthusiast for new talents.

Zeca Assumpção: "I had to adapt not only to this samba but to the way of playing within the Radamés group that had Perrone's way of playing, he (Perrone) did the melodies on the drums. I met Radamés through Sergio Saraceni, who was a composer musician from Globo etc. They were friends, he, Radamés and Didier Luita (Aluisio Didier), and through them I became friends with Radamés, but not of playing and of going in bar to drink beer. I was playing at People's club at that time and one day they came there at night, Radamés and Sérgio, they listened to me play and everything. The next day I went to meet them again for a beer and Radamés said: "Zeca, don't you want to play in my set that we are putting together, the quintet? I would like you to play with me". I answered: Radamés, I don't play with you because I don't know how to play your music, you play a cry that I never actually played! I find it difficult for me! And he said: "Then you will learn". After that I was "forced" to play with him, I was scared to death because I knew it was difficult, but he and all the rest of the group were very patient with me, they had the patience to learn and study, rehearse, and repeat here and repeat there, and so on. I played, it was a great pleasure to play with Radamés and the original group, I was making Vidal's place".

Pedro Vidal Ramos was undoubtedly the bassist who recorded most in the Radio Age. The group to which he belonged, which was generally the basis of all Radamés' orchestrations, was so integrated that he recorded one record (Long Play of 40 minutes) in the afternoon on labels such as Continental and Odeon almost every day, and Henrique Cazes explains why.

Henrique Cazes: "the truth is that when Radamés opens Radio Nacional in 1936 it already has this base trio, piano, bass and drums and will play with this formation in everything. All the recordings until the end of the fifties... the end of the fifties has a point outside the curve which is the record "Paulo Moura Interpreta Radamés", which is another bassist (on the back cover of the record appears only as Paulo) who is a bit of a thing of the time, that time already wanting to be half Bossa-Nova".

Meanwhile, a small revolution was taking place in the suburbs. Several musicians interviewed pointed to one of the vectors that "normalized" the way of playing the carioca genres, and its name was: Maestro Joaquim Antônio Langsdorf Naegle, who had a music school in the neighborhood of Méier and taught, along with his children, drums, double bass, brass instruments, among others. He was a teacher of musicians such as bassist Luiz Alves, drummer Bituca, drummer Dazinho, among many others. His importance even led FUNARTE to make a study about his life.

> **Wilson Das Neves:** "Bituca took me to the school where he studied that was there in the Méier district (north zone of Rio de Janeiro), on 27 Visconde de Tocantins street, Professor Joaquim Naegle[70]".

> **Luiz Alves** "Then I started to get interested in studying and I went to study at Joaquim Naegle's school".

> **Dazinho:** "I went to study with Professor Joaquim who was there in Méier, on Tocantins Street there in Méier".

> **Wilson Das Neves:** "He was a teacher of many people[71]: Bituca, Edison Machado studied there too, Darcy da Cruz of the trumpet, a lot of musicians studied with him. But when I started studying with Joaquim I didn't go to the dance with Bituca to dance, I already put a chair and sat next to him with the orchestra of Permínio Gonçalves in the association of the employees of the commerce, there in Rio Branco Avenue, in the centre".

About Bituca:

> **André "Boxexa" Santos:** "The Bituca that I met and with whom I lived and studied, the great Edgar Nunes Rocca, is an undeniable reference in the drums and percussion of Rio de Janeiro and Brazil".

> **Saulo Bezerra (bassist):** "Bituca, I admired him very much, because he had a class to play, he played like this, it seemed that he traveled on the cymbals, already Wilson das Neves was that scrabble, he let go of the hand of everything that is way. Now Bituca... he looked like he was sewing things together, impressive the way he played".[72]

> **André "Boxexa" Santos:** "besides Bituca's book #1, a green and yellow book called Ritmos Brasileiros e Seus Instrumentos de Percussão, then came #2 which is the

---

[70] The teacher and conductor Joaquim Antônio Langsdorf Naegle (1899-1986) and his children had a school in the suburbs and taught various instruments such as bass, guitar, percussion and wind.

[71] According to the experience of drummer Kleberson Caetano, Joaquim Naegle's classes were chaotic, "everyone played at the same time and he was shouting what to do in the middle of that mess". - interview recorded on April 15, 2017.

[72] Interview filmed with bassist Saulo Bezerra, son of the also legendary bassist Gabriel Bezerra who acted in recordings such as the album COISAS by Moacyr Santos, Sivuca, Jackson do Pandeiro, etc, on April 15, 2016 in Rio de Janeiro.

drums book: Bateria, Método Moderno e Prático, with the orange and yellow cover. They are the numbers 1 and 2 of the Brazilian School of Music, then came the one of mandolin, the one of seven strings guitar, of cavaquinho of Henrique Cazes, Luiz Otávio Braga, and many others".

3.4 The Samba Cruzado

Samba Cruzado, Cruzado for having to cross the upper limbs, was the next step for drummers, and bassists, from the 1940s-50s, and for Brazilian music - the first was traditional samba, transcribed in the Bituca style at the beginning of this chapter. It was nothing more than a "translation" of what was being done in the Samba Schools at that time, in the late 1940s, for the drums. Some attribute its creation to Jadir de Castro[73], but the first notation of this genre was by Edgar Nunes Rocca, the Bituca.

Figure 16: Bituca's Samba Cruzado - years 1940 to 1960.

Wilson Das Neves: "But that traditional samba is very difficult to play (refers to the crossed samba), you see that nobody plays there anymore, because it is difficult, it is not easy for you to coordinate (motorily the members), the Hildofredo (Correia) played like this, Jadir de Castro played like this, Crown... they are the drummers I remember... Sut, Sutinho, Bituca, of course, Plínio Araújo, Cremildo... who else... Mosque, they were the drummers I saw playing like this, there were several, everybody played like this, each one giving his own way of playing, for example: Hildofredo played ONE and ONE, "punsquipunsqui", Bituca played ONE and TWO and I played TWO and TWO. I went to create mine because Professor Joaquim (Naegle) said to me: "listen to everyone, see everyone and take yours".

Oscar "Bolão" Pelon: "This crossed samba story was of Jadir de Castro, there were four guys: Seu Jadir de Castro, Hildofredo Correia, Edgar Nunes Rocca (Bituca) and Wilson das Neves. His Jadir before passing away I talked to him, he said that Eliseu, percussionist, missed work, stayed that hole, and he had to turn himself so it occurred to him to do this: do something more constant in the box and he did (crossing his arms) the deaf with his left hand, that's why it's called cruzado, because I crossed like this, I'm fat and that's why I can't do it. He touched the deaf, one touch stuck and the other released, as if he was really deaf (deaf from Samba School is much bigger). Then Hildofredo Correia, who was very close to Jadir, started to do the first half in the high tone and the second in the deaf (low tone), then: pim (high) pom (low), and in the box was in the rim the division similar to the tambourine, and the bumbo was already that

---

[73] Jadir de Castro (Campos 1927 - Cabo Frio 2015) drummer who started his artistic career at the age of 14, playing as a drummer in the Grande Orquestra da Rádio Clube do Brasil - source: Dicionário Cravo Albin da Música Popular Brasileira.

double bumbo (punctuated eighth note more semicolcheia or semicolline punctuated more cocheira if written in a wing soon): pum, pum-pum, pum-pum... then came Bituca who made the variation I like the most: one in the acute, one in the grave and two in the acute, pim, pom, pim-pum... and Wilson das Neves came making: two in the acute and two in the grave, pim=pim, pom-pom, etc. So there are four versions of this crossed samba business, do you understand?".

Along with the Samba Cruzado comes the Double Lead, the rhythmic figure of a punctuated eighth note plus a repeated "ad aeternum" semicolcheia, hated by the traditional samba dancers coming from regionals and loved by those who would come to be part of the next movement, the Bossa-Nova. The curious thing is that many musicians who started before Bossa- Nova don't make that rhythmic figure, one of them was Tom Jobim himself, which we will see in the next chapter.

André "Boxexa" Santos: "from what he (Bituca) told me and I had the opportunity to hear from other people really Hildofredo Korea would be the comrade who started to put the two beats on the pedal of the bass drum. Maybe in the time that needed to save a deaf person, finally the origin of the drums is a little bit around if you go there in the past".

Oscar "Bolão" Pelon: "It seems to me that they attribute the double bass to Hildofredo, I don't know when Hildofredo did it, but I have a 1947 recording that Manoel Chagas, Sutinho (1931-2005) in a Rádio Nacional song, Pixinguinha's drum concert, Sutinho starts to do a solo and there is that figure: pum-pum, pum-pum, pum-pum... I think they used a lot for solos, to sustain the "thing" of the solo because in the driving there wasn't much that, that comes later (in Bossa-Nova). Now, it is a very interesting rhythmic figure, you can even do a thesis on it, punctuated eighth note more semicolchea, if you go in the basses of Ernesto Nazareth is there: pim, pom-pom, pom-pom, pom-pom. If you see the deaf's way of playing you do two is it here once again. Now, in fact, Luciano Perrone, whom I have seen a lot of playing, he **FEW USED** the bass!

4. BOSSA NOVA AND THE 1970S[74]

Figure 17: Bossa-Nova (Bituca).

The Bossa Nova! Once, in a Master Class I taught at the College of Charleston - SC - USA, a student asked me: "who was the greatest bassist of Bossa-Nova? I stopped and thought a lot, after all how to define "the greatest bassist"? What played best? Subjective! What defined a different path than before? Equally subjective! What else did you record? But where can these numbers be found? What else did you touch on the world's most famous recordings? Yes, that is relevant. The musician who recorded the most in phonograms that are heard around the world until today was the bassist who recorded with Tom Jobim in the United States, who recorded the albums *Wave* (1967 A&M Records), Stone *Flower (1970* CTI Records), Tide (1970 A&M Records), Matita *Perê (1973 A&M Records)*, Urubu (1975 *Warner)* and even the *Brazilian* Antonio, *from 1994,* a little before his death, by A&M Records. After a brief pause I answered: Ron Carter.

How could an American represent Bossa Nova in the rhythm section? Simple: the culture is often cyclical, retrophagistic, and sometimes surprising, as we will see in our interviewees' statements.

I do not go into the story of Tom Jobim because he, based on the research and statements collected here, has little to do with the rhythmic changes that were appearing. His most direct participation was as a great arranger and composer attentive to the changes that were taking place. One of the greatest proofs of this was the virtuous patience he had to deal with the problematic guitarist João Gilberto, seeing in him a kind of "necessary evil" that would add value to his productions, as Sérgio Cabral describes:

> "Then was the battle of arrangement. Tom including all the instruments he thought necessary and John wanting to reduce them. "You're so dumb, Tonzinho!", accused the singer and guitarist, while the composer and arranger swallowed dry. "It was a

---

[74]This chapter of the documentary can be seen at: < https://www.youtube.com/watch?v=-vbSQAtZ8LI&feature=youtu.be>.

very important exercise of patience for me, because I knew that, at that moment, João Gilberto was a fundamental person for my formation as a musician," Tom Jobim would confide many years later to his friends Eduardo "Susto"Athayde and Marco Antônio Bompet (CABRAL, 2015).[75]

I start then with the eternal stir whether Bossa Nova is Samba or another genre.

Wilson Das Neves: "Bossa-Nova is Samba! Everybody speaks Bossa-Nova, Bossa-Nova, Bossa-Nova... is Samba". IBIDEM.

Oscar "Bolão" Pelon: "then 'negozinho' gets crazy with me when I say that Bossa-Nova is not Samba... because Samba for me is batuque[76], man! Of course Bossa-Nova comes from Samba, she's a Samba accent, but SAMBA? Samba has to be batucada! If not Samba!" IBIDEM.

Paulo Sá: "Regarding what Wilson das Neves says, that "everything is Samba", if we make a projection on the previous perspective Pixinguinha, that at that time everything was Polca, it is interesting to observe these perspectives of analysis, the Animal do Cavaquinho himself, Alexandre Gonçalves Pinto, author of the book *O Choro: Reminiscences of the Ancient Weepers,* put Polca as a Brazilian genre, we are perplexed to hear certain statements, but in the historical context this makes a lot of sense: everything is Samba! Nowadays you say that everything is Samba can make sense in terms of interpretation because Choro, for example, already has a hybridism, an involvement with Samba, which is undeniable. The percussion itself. This evolution is what calls attention: before everything was Polka and today everything is Samba!" IBIDEM

Gildásio Paiva, the Dazinho: "... in the 1950's the Bossa-Nova movement began to emerge and at that time I was working at Sacha's, a very famous nightclub at the time - it was from Arakém. There I worked in K. Ximbinho, Júlio, Cipó, Lauro Miranda, Lauro Araújo, Zighetti... I was at Sacha's for nine years. Months later there was the fire at the Boate Vogue, where I had played a little bit too, Vogue was over. I stayed nine years at Sacha's and the club lasted ten, me and Cipó stayed until the end, Cipó stayed another year and left. At Sacha's there was a "deal" that they say was Edison Machado[77] who 'launched', I can't say either, but if it wasn't him he went close to him, playing with his left hand low on the 'box' and his right hand on the *hi-hat*. I listened at the club and couldn't see - because of the low hand - how this guy does to play? - I wondered - what does he do with his hands? That's when I found out that the low left hand was touching the rim of the box and the right hand was doing the *hi-hat* samba. Then Bossa-Nova appeared".

---

[75] Book quote: **Antonio Carlos Jobim: A biography** - Cabral, Sérgio (post 1985-1989). Lazuli. Kindle edition.

[76] Batucada Brazilian term, s. f.., pl. = 'batucadas'. Playing rhythms to accompany songs and informal songs and using "skin" instruments plus, "rattles" or percutating on tables, "matchboxes", drinks bottles and any nearby object, played with "hands", coins, pens, etc. It can also mean the rhythm made by organized "instrumentalists" playing popular pieces, especially the "samba", of which it has become synonymous. In Spanish the equivalent term can be "tamboreo". See also "batuque", batucajé Membr. perc., s. m., pl- quote from: **Dicionário de Percussão** (2002) - D. Frungillo - Editora Unesp - p 36.

[77] Edison Machado (Rio de Janeiro 1934 - 1990) was a very active drummer in the whole Era of Bossa-Nova - see annex of photos - Figure nº17 - Edison Machado - 1957 - MIS - Boate Sacha's.

Figure 18: Edison Machado, 1957 (MIS). Sacha's nightclub.

Incredible is the diversity of versions that each musician who was performing at the time has of how the Bossa-Nova movement emerged. Many times gender and movement get confused. It wasn't obviously a static thing that suddenly sprang up, it was the result of years of evolution of mannerisms, many of them linked to the rhythm section both from the radios and the recordings during the period.

Paulo Sá: "What I have to say about Tom Jobim[78] is that he always spoke: "this tendency is there in the air, it's who to take first", this tendency was formed exactly by the practice of some musicians at that moment".

Roberto Menescal: "I don't remember the first recording, but I remember the first test, I had Aloysio de Oliveira[79] who was a producer and lived in the USA and had a

---

[78] The pianist, composer and arranger Antonio Carlos Brasileiro de Almeida Jobim, or just Tom Jobim (Rio 1927 - NY 1994). "Antonio Carlos Jobim was born on January 25, 1927, a Tuesday at 11:15 p.m. ("11:00 p.m. and a quarter"), on Rua Conde de Bonfim, 634 ("I am from the time when one was born at home," said Tom), Freguesia do Engenho Velho, that is, in Tijuca. Before, the family lived in Copacabana, but financial problems forced the move to Tijuca, where the rent was cheaper". Quote from the book *Antonio Carlos Jobim: A biography* of Sérgio Cabral (pos 156-158). Lazuli. Kindle edition.

[79] Aloysio de Oliveira (Rio de Janeiro 1914 - Los Angeles 1995) "Aloysio had been living in the United States since 1939, when he embarked as a member of the Bando da Lua ensemble to accompany Carmen Miranda's performances in that country. After Carmen's death in August 1955, he was waiting for a job opportunity to return definitively to Brazil. The first invitation came from businessman Victor Costa, owner of radio and television stations in Rio de Janeiro and São Paulo, to produce programs on TV Paulista, Canal 5. Four days after arriving in São Paulo in March 1956 and watching several programs on Brazilian television, Aloysio informed Victor Costa that this was not the work to which he would like to dedicate himself. The conversation resulted in an invitation to produce and present a programme on Mayrink Veiga Radio in Rio de Janeiro, with retransmission to Rádio Nacional de São Paulo. Thus, the programme *Se a lua contouse (If the Moon Told),* sponsored by Sal de Fruta Eno and Emulsão de Scott, presented by Aloysio and the singer Aurora Miranda, Carmen's sister, with the participation of Vadico in the musical part. The programme lasted exactly one month. In May, Aloysio de Oliveira accepted the

vocal ensemble, and he came to Brazil and started bringing some things, American news, Aloysio stayed close to ten years there, and in the middle of Hollywood, so he had a different vision of us, more advanced. And when he came he went to work at Odeon and "had" André Midani[80] who is this person who came from France in the early 1960s - late 1950s - and changed a lot of things in Brazilian music, helped a lot with modern Brazilian music, and André used to go to the little meetings that we did at Nara Leão's house, they were still very amateur meetings, everybody playing their guitar, and one day André said: "don't you want to do a test there at Odeon?"I said, "Oh, man," and he said, "All of a sudden we're recording a record, but let's take a test! So it was me and a little group: bass, piano, drums, a pistom, and I know we went for the test and there was Aloysio de Oliveira, the conductor Oswaldo Borba... so in the technique, and we saw those figures in a suit, it scared... boy! My hand was not in the guitar, it was a failure! We didn't manage to record anything, it was a failure, we left defeated of there! But a little later André prepared us and we made another test where I made the first recording, a little floppy disk that was called "Bossa is Bossa", something like that".

Henrique Cazes: "Aloysio is a guy who comes naturally with the experience he had accumulated over the years in the US and he feels that there is a more modern trend, and that more modern trend is that he will dominate the label's catalogue and he will be the guy who will help this "block in the street", including with young musicians like the Menescal ensemble and others more. I think he as a producer helped transform that into a product, but the musical transformation was already being experienced[81]".

In a retrospective of the life of drummer Wilson das Neves, André Tandeta sums up the progression of the socio-cultural tendencies that "ended up" in the era of the Bossa Nova from the 1950s to the 1960s.

André Tandeta (drummer and teacher): "Das Neves he started studying drums when he was already 18 years old, he said that when he started the dances he did they were far away, in Irajá and others, and he came to the South Zone until he arrived in Copacabana".

4.1 Bossa-Nova, the Majors and the "influence of jazz".

---

invitation formulated by Douglas Reed, director of Odeon, to take the place of Antonio Carlos Jobim, a name, by the way, that he had never heard of. But Tom knew him very well as a radio listener, as he was a fan of the Moon Gang. They were introduced to each other at the cocktail party promoted by Odeon so that Odeon employees could meet their new artistic director. "It's good that you've arrived," said Tom during the presentation. Quote from the book: *Antonio Carlos Jobim: A biography* of Sérgio Cabral (pos 1243-1254). Lazuli. Kindle edition.

[80] Andre Midani (Sira 1932) was president of Odeon, Phillips do Brasil and Phonogram among others.

[81] In Radamés Gnattali's statement to the Museu da Imagem e do Som, Hermínio Bello de Carvalho remembered the name of composer Valzinho as one of the modernizers of Brazilian popular music. Then, a dialogue was established exactly about the pioneers of bossa nova: "*Jairo Severiano - Valzinho knew music. By the way, he didn't know, but he did all those ninth, eleventh, thirteenth chords, he did everything. Tom Jobim - Sweet poison that says it, right? Dark glasses... Jairo - All this in a time when few people did it. Tom - It was the staff of National Radio. Radamés - I think they were the ones who started bossa nova. Tom: Yeah, let's say they were the basis of that section. Hermínio - Boy, Valzinho. Tom - Boy, Valzinho, Radamés... Hermínio - Custódio Mesquita. Tom - Custódio. Hermínio - Later, several people, including people who were forgotten like Johnny Alf. Radamés - But he is alive. Tom - Very good. Radamés - They have certain things that cannot be understood. Jairo - Johnny Alf has good things. Tom - Beautiful, very good.*" - Quote from the book: **Antonio Carlos Jobim: A biography** - Cabral, Sérgio (pos 1617-1625). Lazuli. Kindle edition.

With the failure of the Bay of Pigs Invasion in southern Cuba in April 1961, the United States and its entertainment industry declared what would be the end of the Salsa Age and in its place put partner Brazil to supply the demand for Latin music. It would be the great opportunity of Bossa-Nova, and that opportunity the country did not let pass. It would not be for nothing the concert at Carnegie Hall a little over a year after the incident in Cuba.

> **Roberto Menescal:** "I want to remember first something that was of the utmost importance, man! It was one of the most important things in the new Brazilian music (bossa nova onwards), this I'm talking about in 1957, I was given a record by an American singer called Julie London, *Julie is Her Name* was the name of the record. I said: cool! I asked: what is the orchestra? - no, it's a bass and a guitar, I said: alone?! Because if you look at Ella Fitzgerald and Sarah Vaughan it was all with orchestra behind it, sing: "this can't be love..." "...dum-dum-dum (simulates a rhythm section in the voice)" that dum-dum-dum is everybody there, right? There suddenly it does only: "pom-plim-plim-plim" (it simulates a guitar with the accompaniment of a bass in the voice), everything explained, a bass and a guitar, I said: man what is that! It was the first time that I heard a bass and a guitar explained, then the whole record like this. I went so crazy with what I gathered Baden Powell, Carlinhos Lyra, Durval Ferreira ... everyone who played the guitar and auditioned, everyone went "what the hell, man!" "who is this bassist?" It was Ray but it wasn't Ray Brown, another Ray I forgot his name - Ray Leatherwood (1914 - 1996) - and Barney Kessel[82] who is my idol until today. Then we did it like this, each one chooses a song and in a month's time it has to be "taken". So we got together later and 500 new chords came to the Brazilian music because of this record".

> **Henrique Cazes:** "Barney Kessel came to play at a jazz festival in Brazil, it wasn't Free Jazz, it was a previous one, and they took him to Suvaco de Cobra[83], on a Sunday off, Miúcha took him, he loved it and said he wanted to play, they went back to Miúcha's house and he turned on the guitar in the stereo and played a lot of choro. And then everyone got scared: "but how do you know this?" And he answered: "I lived behind Laurindo Almeida[84], Laurindo taught me, Laurindo taught me a lot of harmony and such. In 1946 when Dutra closes the Urca Casino he gets into a little work here and he goes to the U.S. and in a short time he manages to go as a hired soloist with Stan Kenton's orchestra[85], Laurindo was a very competent guy in the front and Laurindo's trip to the US West Coast had such an impact that he was the guy who recorded the most, who won the most Grammy, who recorded the most film track, we can talk here about the *Godfather, Bonanza,* openings, banjo solo, mandolin solo. Laurindo was also a multi-instrumentalist, he was the Boy's partner - the Boy brings a lot of stuff from the USA - but it was a very fast passage and he went there playing tenor guitar with Carmem Miranda, but Laurindo's experience even with the things he undertakes both in the classical guitar area and in the west coast jazz area, all that... and Laurindo's importance is very underestimated here in Brazil. He doesn't come back to Brazil anymore, he used to come here and play and come back to the USA, I met him one of the times, close to his death, at Radamés' house. Yeah, the interesting thing about the Brazilian who thinks the influence comes from there, when in fact a

---

[82] Barney Kessel (1923 - 2004) was an American *jazz* guitarist (Figure 20).

[83] Suvaco de Cobra group of crying and place of crying wheels.

[84] Laurindo Almeida (1917 - 1995). Laurindo José de Araújo Almeida Nóbrega Neto (Miracatu 1917 - Los Angeles 1995) was a Brazilian guitarist, mandolinist and composer. Throughout his career he received 5 Grammy Awards. The guitarist won an Oscar for composing the soundtrack for the short animation *The Magic Pear Tree*. (Figure 21)

[85] Stan Kenton (1911 - 1979) was a West Coast Jazz musician and his orchestra was one of the most famous in the 1950s and 1960s.

part of it there, a part like that, even though it was so friendly to Brazilian music, wasn't friendly by chance, it's because he left here and came back".

Figure 19: Barney Kessel.

Figure 20: Laurindo Almeida.

4.2 Gabriel Bezerra: one of the pioneers of the Swinging Language

Sérgio Barrozo (bassist): "Look, the bassists I remember crossing in the studio were Vidal (Pedro Vidal Ramos), who was the oldest of all, then there was Gabriel Bezerra, who was a very funny guy because he talked to me, but he was super shy, but he said some funny things. Even the first best bass I bought I commented with him: "well Gabriel, this bass is not sounding" and he replied: "wait! You have to be calm, the sound will "come out" - I heard everything they were talking about".

Saulo Bezerra (bassist): "All his name was Gabriel Bezerra de Mello, he started in Recife playing the trumpet, a young man who supported his family by playing. He learned music from Sivuca, they learned it together, he was Sivuca's partner for all I know. My father didn't tell me much and he was always a quiet guy".

Roberto Menescal: "Gabriel was always there in the studios, quiet with his bass at hand. He read everything, everything first-class, he was a great reader".

51

Omar Cavalheiro: "What I heard about Gabriel was that he was part of the Globo Network orchestra and the only reference even that I have is a comment from Luizão Maia[86], we were at the Centro Cultural Banco do Brasil and I asked: "did you know Gabriel?" and he answered: "When Gabriel "appeared" in Rio de Janeiro was something compared to Nico Assumpção[87]".

Saulo Bezerra: "Gabriel arrived here in the 1950s and started playing with Copinha[88] and Steve Bernard[89], it was Steve Bernard and his ensemble, were formations that in the case of Steve Bernard was a quintet and Copinha that already had a little bigger formation. He even played with Ary Barroso too, he played with a lot of people, he played with all the foreign artists that came here. He played in the beginning of TV Tupi my father was an employee of TV Tupi. He was the guy who recorded *Coisas*, by Moacir Santos, the first record, he recorded (with Wilson das Neves on drums). And that recently they made the *Ouro Negro* with the bass lines all repeated on the LP *Coisas*".

Sandrino Santoro: "From Gabriel I remember a story at the Maracanãzinho that had the International Song Festival. Once I was called to do and I only had music to "play with my finger" (*pizzicato*) and only chords ciphered these things. In the first rehearsal I was like this... I said: "oh my god! I won't play anything!" and I didn't play, so I got close to Gabriel and said: "Gabriel...." he said: "no Sandrino, that plays (the fundamental ones) with the bow, a little bit, and the next day I started playing with the bow and I liked the thing, and the singer I was accompanying said to me: "look, it's *pizzicato*!", and Gabriel said: "no, no, I'm the one who makes the *pizzicato* he makes the bow! So it was such a wonderful night and I ended up doing the Festival".

4.3 The Double Bass in Tom Jobim and Bossa-Nova: Rise and fall of the electric bass

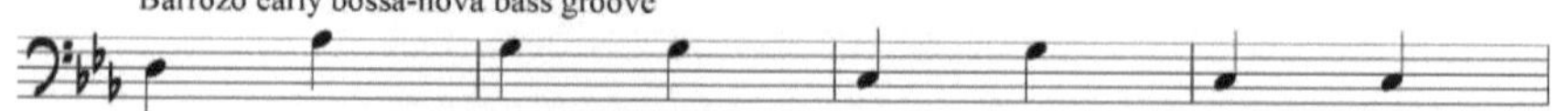

Figure 21: Sérgio Barrozo's Bossa-Nova - 1960s.

In April 1954, Tom Jobim's name first appeared on a Continental record label. He preferred to be identified as Antonio Carlos Jobim and would fight some more time for the record companies to forget his nickname Tom. Until Ary Barroso warned him: "This is a lost cause, an English fight. Who will call him Antonio Carlos, if Tom is much simpler? (CABRAL, 2015).[90]

---

[86] Luiz Oliveira da Costa Maia, known as Luizão Maia (Rio de Janeiro 1949 - Tokyo 2005) was a Brazilian bassist and composer who revolutionized the way of playing electric bass in Samba. He became famous from his recordings with the group of César Camargo Mariano who accompanied singer Elis Regina for almost a decade.

[87] Nico Assumpção, artistic name of Antônio Álvaro Assumpção Neto, (1954 - 2001) was a Brazilian bassist who took the technique of the instrument to a new level in the 1970s.

[88] Nicolino Copia, known as Copinha (São Paulo 1910 - Rio de Janeiro 1984), was a Brazilian composer, flutist, clarinettist and saxophonist who stood out in Choro and had several ensembles between the 1950s and 1980s in Rio de Janeiro.

[89] Steve Bernard was the name of Stephen Bernhardt (Romania 1915 - unknown) was a Romanian organist, pianist, orchestra leader and composer, who settled in Brazil in 1952.

[90] Quote from the book: **Antonio Carlos Jobim: Uma biografia**, de Sérgio Cabral (p. 998-1001). Lazuli. Kindle edition.

Bossa-Nova is one in Tom Jobim's recordings and another in the "Menescal class" records. Among these young musicians of the late 1950's, the bassist Sérgio Barrozo was one of those who shared here his great experience of these first recordings. Besides Roberto Menescal to the electric guitar, the group counted on João Palma to the drums (later it was Edison Machado), Henri to the flute and Eumir Deodato, with 18 years of age, to the piano and in the arrangements.

Sérgio Barrozo himself wrote the bass line (Figure 22) as the "levada" of the Bossa-Nova of the early years and then wrote what would be "today", or more precisely what would come later in the 1970s (always on top of a harmony of a cadence of IIm - V7 - IMaj7):

Figure 22: Bossa Nova bass line - 1970s.

This difference was basically the "water divisor" of the aesthetics that had already been happening in the nucleus Radamés and Tom Jobim with the bassists Pedro Vidal Ramos and Gabriel Bezerra - with the drummers Luciano Perrone, Bituca and Wilson das Neves - and what would be recorded by the class of composers Roberto Menescal and Carlinhos Lyra with a more "jazzy" bass and the drums with the "Samba nos Pratos" - attributed to the drummer Ediso Machado[91].

Adriano Giffoni[92] (bassist and author): "So I could see one thing about Tom Jobim that the bass of Tom Jobim's tunes are much simpler than the bass of a song by Carlos Lyra or Menescal or another artist (from Bossa-Nova). The system he used was the bass, but in a seminimum".[93]

Sérgio Barrozo: "I used to play Jazz, a lot of Jazz... I tried to play Jazz because if you can't imagine it at that time until today. We started trying to use Jazz conduction in

---

[91] Drummer Kleberson Caetano tells the story that Edison Machado had the skin of his box pierced in the middle of a job and only "left" to him was the option to touch his right hand on the *Hi-Hat* and his left hand on the rim of the box. Interview recorded on April 27, 2017.

[92] Adriano Giffoni is a bassist and author of several methods for the instrument besides having ten authorial CDs recorded.

[93] Interview filmed with bassist Adriano Giffoni on the afternoon of December 8, 2016 in Tijuca neighborhood, Rio de Janeiro

Brazilian music so much that you see even *walking bass*[94] playing Samba, and it was a totally American thing with a Brazilian sauce. That was interesting, and it started to happen in the 1960s until 1970s. The trios played like that, so much that it appeared, I don't like that nomenclature, but Samba Jazz appeared, which was a freer way to play, you already played until giving notes out of rhythm, then really the bass had an evolution in Brazilian music.

These same lines written by the bassist Augusto Mattoso[95] in the perception of what were the first lines of Bossa-Nova.

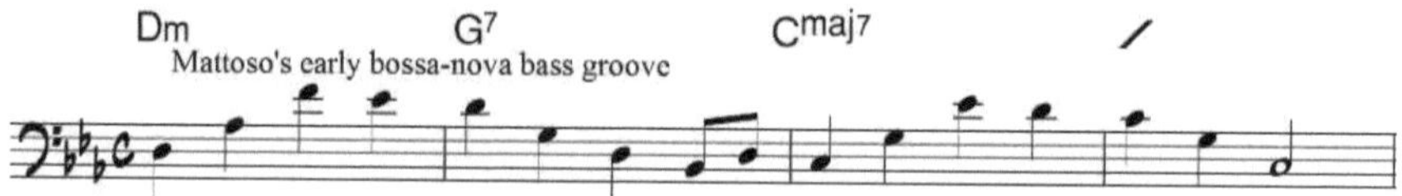

Figure 23: Augusto Mattoso's Bossa-Nova - 1960s.

Augusto Mattoso: "What was done in the past was quite different from what happens today. What do you mean? The bassists, for example, they played in a simpler way, like a *walking bass*, a *walking* Samba, they played everything one note at a time. There were some details, for example the drum bass played more on the second *beat*. With the advent of modernity, the electric bass, I don't know exactly where that changed, but the drum bass turned into that business (double bass seen in the previous chapter): tum, tum, tum. And with the advent of the electric bass the guys started playing along with the bass, so it became a take like this:"[96]

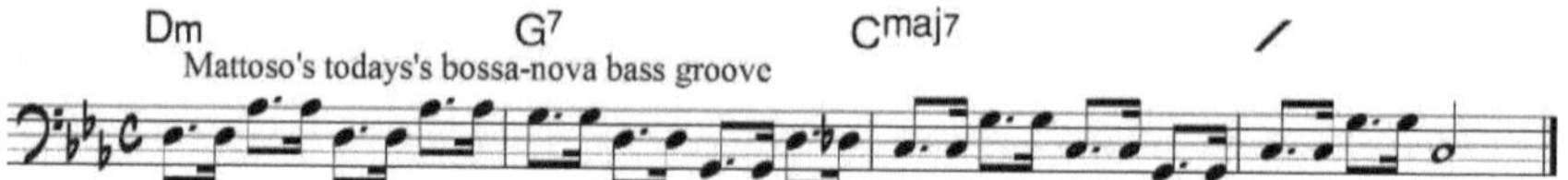

Figure 24: Augusto Mattoso's Bossa-Nova - 1970s and today.

---

[94] *Walking bass* is the driving used by Jazz bassists for the serious counterpoint. In the words of Educator Mark Gridley in his book Jazz Styles:
"The bassist improvises his part in the rhythm section by plucking a string once per beat and occasionally adding embellishments. Many bassists play the second and fourth of every four notes harder than the first and third. This helps create swing feeling. The bass pattern often rises and falls as though the music is walking up and down a staircase. This timekeeping style is called walking bass. Good walking bass lines make musical sense by themselves. In fact, some soloists consider walking bass to be the most essential sound in the rhythm section. They would play without drums or chording instrument before they would play without walking bass."
Translation:"The bassist improvises his part in the rhythm section by playing in *pizzicato* a note once every time and occasionally adding ornaments. Many bassists play the second and fourth of every four notes with more pressure than the first and third. This helps to create a swinging sensation. The bass lines often go up and down scales as if the music was walking up and down a staircase. This style of levada is called walking bass. The good walking bass lines make the musical sense for you. In fact, some soloists consider walking *bass to be* the most important sound in the rhythm section. They would play without drums or harmonic instruments, but never without the bass". Quote from: **Jazz Styles: History and Analysis** - Gridley, Mark (2017). (pos 868-869). Pearson Education, Inc. Kindle edition.
[95] Augusto Mattoso is a bassist and composer with three CDs of Brazilian Jazz/Music and an international career.
[96] Interview filmed with bassist Augusto Mattoso on the morning of 12 April 2016 at the Botanical Garden, Rio de Janeiro.

Many have argued that Bossa-Nova would not be a genre, nor a sub-genre of Samba, but rather a movement. Academically, we cannot escape this definition of a musical genre, but we can understand why the thought of being an ideological movement once we consider the diversity of rhythmic incisors in the serious counterpoint, observed in this research, which is even frightening. There was no mannerist normalization because it was obviously a matter of readings and re-reading by various artists of different formations with an age jump of almost one generation among themselves, which is the case of Tom Jobim who, in 1962, the date of the recording of the album *Bossa is Bossa* of Roberto Menescal's class, was 35 years old and the young arranger of these phonograms, Eumir Deodato, would still be 19 years old.

The search for novelties to launch in the market made the record companies open space for these new mannerisms, experienced producers like Aloysio de Oliveira and André Midani, very skillfully created market in the younger sectors absorbing these new talented musicians. Adding all this to the technological innovations in the area of luthiery and recording that were arriving in Brazil, the languages of Samba and Bossa-Nova would change a lot.

According to *The free online encyclopedia of Washington state history*, the electric bass was invented much earlier, in 1930 by Paul Tutmarc[97] in Seattle in the United States and improved in the 1950s by Leo Fender, but in Brazil the "novelty" would not arrive until the early 1960s. It was a technology that facilitated clarity in Brazilian recordings, which were still made two-channel studios until 1974, and still solved the issue of tuning, or the lack of it, because they were "tempered" instruments based on mirrors with frets, such as the guitar, and with a much simpler mechanics than the predecessor acoustic bass, so the electric bass still made it possible to issue more notes.

Still defending the idea of an ideological movement, we can cite as an example that Bossa Nova launched names like João Donato[98], a young accordionist and acrean pianist who, instead of the influence of genres like Samba, his music brought a cultural "baggage" more linked to the Caribbean and Cuban Salsa.

> **Adriano Giffoni:** "Then I had the opportunity to play with João Donato, that mixture of Samba with Latin music, with Cha-cha-cha, with Salsa. João doesn't like me to play traditional Samba. He likes this thing of the always anticipated eighth note".
>
> **Luiz Alves (bassist):** "O Donato[99], for example, this beat that he does for the Cuban side more, Latin music, that fits the Samba".

---

[97] Quote from the site: <http://www.historylink.org/File/7479>.
[98] João Donato de Oliveira Neto (Rio Branco 1934) is a Brazilian pianist, accordionist, arranger, singer and composer who arrived in Rio de Janeiro in 1945.
[99] Luiz Alves still plays with João Donato.

Roberto Menescal: "There was still a lot of acoustic bass playing (in 1962) because the trios came a lot with the acoustic bass, even for the beauty of the instrument. I have the impression that in that recording (of the album *Bossa is Bossa*) it was still acoustic bass, still. The electric basses came a lot in the *shows*, in the dances. It was good to take - apart from the amplifier - it played sitting down, the people liked very much to play sitting down, the acoustic could not. So the change was very big in the years 1963 around. I think it changed everything, man! And thanks to God it has!".

Sérgio Barrozo: "When they started going in as an electric bass the guys thought it was wonderful, because the electric bass would go straight on the studio table and it didn't even have a *direct box and it*[100] would take out a "ready" sound, it didn't have that acoustic thing, that problem, so much so that already in the middle of the 1950's I had to buy an electric bass and migrate to the electric bass. And from then on I started to record almost everything on the electric bass (speaks with regret). I recorded ten percent acoustic and the rest was just electric bass".

Wilson das Neves: "Yes, but as soon as he (Barrozo) managed to make independence, the studio, he left there because he said it was electric ukulele".

Sergio Barrozo: "Back in the late 1960s, when Tom Jobim went to the United States and recorded those records on his famous ones, the bassist was Ron Carter, and Ron Carter was a guy who really had a defined sound and played the most harmonic thing even though his rhythm was a little Americanized, but he came up with a new language and that influenced everybody, of course, because he played a clear bass, It was easy to hear what he was doing and even American music recorded bass (acoustic) very well since the 1950s, you hear bassists who were excellent like Paul Chambers who did solos that you listened to, of course it's not like today, but you understand his solo, he did bow solos, but actually this modernization of the bass language in Brazilian music may have changed a bit from Ron Carter. If you compare it to the 1930s and the 40s and 50s, even at the time I started recording it was much better recorded, in the old recordings you don't define a note, you're even in doubt: do you have a double bass there? But not as early as the 1960s, you listened to the bass, you played according to your limitations, but you came and listened. I have recordings of that time that you listen to. So much so that later in 1965 I recorded with Don Salvador and Edison Machado a trio called *Rio 65 Trio*, the bass sound is not excellent but you already define the notes, you have bass solos is a simpler thing, but it started to improve there".

Henrique Cazes: "Then we will have to take into consideration a technological issue, the electric double bass undergoes a radical improvement in the 1960s. You can see that the electric double bass was a bit of a "like that" business and soon good instruments with sound, with bass, with body and with good amplifiers will begin to appear. It is a technological change. Luizão Maia used this technological change and used this weight that the technological change brought to put this accent (in the second half), because in fact this accent is almost a return to the Samba of the 1930s, because it has to do with. It will make this character of the most sambada thing, the deaf thing, and in the deaf thing the accent is in the second half. He will use it with the electric double bass now with a very *punchy* sound, with a lot of weight... so it turns out to be a remarkable thing in the recordings of the singer Elis Regina as the phonogram *É Com Esse Que Eu Vou* (*Elis* Album of 1973) is a perfect example of that, the César Camargo Mariano with that damned swing and the drummer I think is Das Neves, no, it was Paulinho Braga[101], it's a stylistic thing that went very well there in that combination with Rhodes piano, it worked very well. But I think Luizão's wisdom was to use that novelty".

---

[100] *Direct Box* or DI is a small box used in recording studios that transmits the signal from electric and electronic instruments so that it reaches the mixer with the most appropriate impedance and without distortions.

[101] Paulo Braga (1942) is a drummer who took part in most of Elis Regina's recordings and also played with Tom Jobim.

Omar Cavalheiro: "Only then I started to listen to Luizão Maia and he didn't abuse it (the double *beat* on the second *beat*)".

Zeca Assumpção: "I met Luizão at that time, at the time he was playing with Elis Regina, I met him on some occasion and I don't remember exactly which one, I went to see one of their *shows, and* soon after there was a fight between them and Luizão and Braga left the group, and I went to play with Elis Regina acoustic and electric. But playing in Luizão's place was hard, and in fact the band didn't even suck the half that they sucked with Luizão and Braga. So it was hard, it was hard for me this time because it didn't work, I stayed six months with Elis and stopped".

Luiz Alves: "Luizão was the one who played the electric bass making the bass bass (two basses) together with the bass and nowadays after all these things have been developing nowadays the bass plays seminimas, colcheias and is no longer together, the bass and the bass are no longer together".

Augusto Mattoso: "Look, I believe Paul McCartney is totally right when he says that the future is in the 60s and 70s, I would even say more: the future is here inside us and especially today. Today we have a technological apparatus to support us that was unimaginable when we were kids. When you would imagine that you would push a button and see what you wanted, the thing would appear in front of you. We can try to use something that is rare, especially in our country today, that common sense for you to evaluate, to think about what you are doing. In relation to music this is fundamental, you think about what you're doing, what you're going to play, how you're going to play, if you're playing with whom? Osmar Milito? So I'll play more like this (in the old style), if you're going to play in a *rock* band then you take the pick, and if you're going to play something else you have to play according to each situation, learn to play the styles. That was something that Osmar Milito "took a lot on my foot" and he showed me this difference. When you're going to play '40s music it's one thing, you're going to play Bill Evans it's one thing, Chick Corea it's another. If you're going to play a Samba-Song it's something else, everything has a way of playing it. So you've got a lot of references to make your music contrast, so your music isn't a boring thing, with resources and information for you to add to what you're doing that can lead you to make a very interesting song.

CONCLUSION

How do you put the final considerations of a dissertation and documentary of such a large proportion on the Carioca genres? After all it was more than 35 hours of filming with 20 different interviewees that were organized in four episodes of 30 minutes of documentary each, where I could relate the experience of artists still alive. Many of those who were lucky enough to meet the pioneering musicians who were part of the object of all this research, such as Pixinguinha, Radamés Gnattali, Garoto, Bituca, Luciano Perrone, Pedro Vidal Ramos and Gabriel Bezerra, and others who witnessed *in locco* the changes in the way of interpreting the genres. After the documentary set up, I had then the also great work of doing its full text transcription here, always taking care to "try" to explain what the images "say", with the body languages of each one and the inflections of our language that many times the writing leaves to be desired. I would also like to point out that, unfortunately, in this research was registered the last testimony of the drummer Dazinho who died two weeks later. The feeling for those who document something so precious is that it is running against time and cannot fail, because important questions had not yet been answered by those artists who hold a good part of the history of Carioca and Brazilian culture.

The question then becomes more pertinent (how to put the final considerations), because, if I was able to answer so many questions during this process, it became clear that many others appeared and so many remained unanswered - for example: what happened to Pedro Vidal Ramos? We can, through the testimonies, simply state that Vidal was the father of the double bass in Brazilian popular music today and none of the 20 interviewees even knows if he is alive or dead.

I hope that this more modern and dynamic format of research will be repeated a lot with the next researchers to come, about the importance of this kind of work reflects the producer Roberto Menescal:

> **Roberto Menescal:** "Look Lipe, there's something interesting, for example: today we talking here you said: "this I don't know where it came from" "and this I couldn't know" "and how did he die?" "this one etc." Why didn't you do that? I see the following, and it's a very particular opinion, I see how music - so-called modern music[102] - is not in vogue, so loud. So you begin to wonder about history, especially the 1960s and before. In our *concerts* today the producers talk: can you open up after about 15 minutes for the staff to ask? I say: you can! Then I see the curiosity of things that were not there before. Because in the time we used to do it there wasn't, because there was so much going on that the "guy" didn't care to know, today "he" wants to know why it was, how it was and who it was, right? So thanks to these things as you are recording these testimonies, not only mine, but I'm talking about everyone, we're going to leave the story a little bit: what was it and why was it, right?

Carioca rhythms are great representatives of national culture. For Rio de Janeiro, artists from all over Brazil have always converged seeking visibility and work from the Empire until the end of the 1970s, but for those who are still in the market today, the city of Rio de Janeiro is resisting political mistreatment and a succession of terrible cultural guidelines of more than four decades presenting annually a surprising musical renewal and virtuoso musicians who will certainly still bring new ways of playing the Brazilian Rhythms on Double Bass.

---

[102] It refers to popular music after the 1960s.

BIBLIOGRAPHICAL REFERENCES

AZEVEDO, L. C. **Rádio Nacional** (2009). Available at: http://www.fgv.br/cpdoc/acervo/dicionarios/verbete-tematico/radio-nacional. Access: month and year.

CABRAL, Sergio. **Antonio Carlos Jobim: A Biography** - Lazuli. Kindle Edition, 2015.

CARDOSO, André. A Brazilian bass method, from the 19th century (1838): Lino José Nunes. **Brazilian Music Magazine**. Graduate Program of Music - School of Music of UFRJ. Vol. 24, n. 2, p. 437-422 Jul./Dec., 2011.

CASTRO, Ruy. **Carmen Uma Biografia** (2005) - Rio de Janeiro - Companhia das Letras.

CLARK, Fernando. **Professor Guilherme Halfed Fontainha** (1999) - Fontainha - Rio de Janeiro.

DICTIONARY. Groove Dictionary of Music. Translation by Eduardo Francisco Alves Concise Edition, Jorge Zahar Editor, 1994.

FRUNGILLO, D. **Percussion Dictionary**. Unesp Publisher - Official Press. São Paulo, 2002.

GREEN, Barry. **The Mastery of Music: Ten Pathways to True Artistry.** Broadway Books, 2003.

GRIDLEY, Mark. **Jazz Styles: History and Analysis**. - Pearson Education, Inc., 2017.

MILES, Barry. **Many Years From Now**. Londres: Holt Paperbacks, 1p, 1998.

ROCCA, Edgar Nunes - **Brazilian Rhythms and their Percussion Instruments**. Rio de Janeiro - Brazilian School of Music, 1962.

ANNEX 1 - List of Interviewees

61

Adriano Giffoni - Bassist and Author.

André "Boxexa" Santos - Drummer and Professor.

André Cardoso - PhD Professor and Conductor.

André Tandeta - Drummer and Researcher.

Flávio Silva - Musicologist.

Gildário Paiva, the Dadinho - Drummer (*in memoriam*).

Henrique Cazes - Professor.

Luís Filipe Lima - Violinist and Writer.

Luiz Alves - Bassist.

Moacyr Viana Marques da Silva, the Biju - Saxophonist.

Omar Cavalheiro - Professor and Bassist.

Oscar "Bolão" Pelon - Professor and Drummer.

Paulo Henrique Loureiro de Sá - Professor and Bandolinist.

Roberto Menescal - Producer and Guitarist.

Sandrino Santoro - Professor and Bassist.

Saulo Bezerra - Bassist.

Wilson das Neves - Drummer.

Zeca Assumpção - Bassist (one of the members of Radamés).

I want morebooks!

Buy your books fast and straightforward online - at one of world's fastest growing online book stores! Environmentally sound due to Print-on-Demand technologies.

Buy your books online at
www.morebooks.shop

Kaufen Sie Ihre Bücher schnell und unkompliziert online – auf einer der am schnellsten wachsenden Buchhandelsplattformen weltweit! Dank Print-On-Demand umwelt- und ressourcenschonend produziert.

Bücher schneller online kaufen
www.morebooks.shop

KS OmniScriptum Publishing
Brivibas gatve 197
LV-1039 Riga, Latvia
Telefax +371 686 204 55

info@omniscriptum.com
www.omniscriptum.com

Printed by Books on Demand GmbH, Norderstedt / Germany